T0332561

Endorsements

"This practical guide to *Improving Productivity and Service in Depot Businesses* is a must read for any operations manager wanting to improve their professional skills. Colin is undoubtedly the most accomplished operations leader I have ever worked with, and his guide is full of practical tips and tools to help hone and enhance operational management expertise."

David Taylor-Smith, MBE, FRGS, Portfolio Chairman, and Former FTSE 100 Board Director

"The author enables you to clearly understand straightforward methodologies that can be applied piecemeal or holistically, and which will improve operational efficiency. Having applied some of the techniques referenced in the book, I recommend this book and the content."

Warren Edmondson, CEO, The Safegroup Ltd., UK

"I worked with Colin on a successful business turnaround implementing some of the principles included in this book; the project was a success, and the business continues to perform well."

Aiden Harper, BA. M.MUS. MD Ireland

"*Improvig Productivity and Services in Depot Businesses* provides invaluable tried and tested methodologies and practical tools and techniques. Applied correctly they have the ability to transform the performance of a business. The benefits gained from managing non-productive hours were transformational for the business I managed. The techniques described in the operating rhythm (drumbeat) chapter are applicable in any business and is something I still utilise at an executive level."

Kevin O'Connor, MBA, CEO

"I had the opportunity to work with Colin on an important operational project in Colombia, we applied some of the principles presented in the book and achieved strong results. This book is a must for any professional or student working in operations."

Claudio Enrique Pita Garcia, University of Politecnico Grancolumbiano, Columbia

Improving Productivity and Service in Depot Businesses

This book is specifically for working operations managers across the broad range of business types that deploy fleet and product via a myriad of service types. It is applicable to businesses with small medium to large fleets in haulage, 3PL, and any service business operating a depot structure. The book is less about theoretical concepts – although specific references point to theories including Lean, continuous improvement, net promoter score, and balanced scorecard – but is essentially a practical guide applying worked examples and generic templates regarding the core ten activities that are critical to achieving service and profit expectation in any depot, route-based business deploying fleet. Every working manager – front-line to COO – will identify with and grasp that these are fundamental areas and that, if improvement can be sustained, will deliver better service to customers and enhanced profit in both local and business levels. The key areas examined are:

- People management
- Fleet management
- Route scheduling
- Optimisation of non-productive (on-depot) time
- Driver debrief
- Customer service and complaint management and measurement
- Key performance indicators
- The operating rhythm
- Continuous improvement

Improving Productivity and Service in Depot Businesses

How Haulage, 3PL, and Service Companies Can Increase Quality and Customer Satisfaction

Colin Woodland

Routledge
Taylor & Francis Group

A PRODUCTIVITY PRESS BOOK

First published 2023
by Routledge
605 Third Avenue, New York, NY 10158

and by Routledge
4 Park Square, Milton Park, Abingdon, Oxon, OX14 4RN

Routledge is an imprint of the Taylor & Francis Group, an informa business

ISBN: 978-1-032-34782-0 (hbk)
ISBN: 978-1-032-34781-3 (pbk)
ISBN: 978-1-003-32382-2 (ebk)

DOI: 10.4324/9781003323822

Typeset in Garamond
by Deanta Global Publishing Services, Chennai, India

Contents

Preface

This practical guide is written for operations managers working in the UK within the Haulage, 3PL, or any route-based service-sector business deploying commercial van (LCVs) and or heavy goods (HGV) vehicle fleets; the content will also prove insightful to post-graduate students studying road-transport logistics. Core operational management disciplines are pertinent to all route-based businesses, irrespective of the service performed; and through worked examples together with proven methodologies, the aim of this book is to provide operational managers with guidelines that will aid improvement of service to customers, increase efficiency and productivity, and enhance profit. The author has successfully embedded these core principles in several businesses achieving sustained cost benefit in the range of 8%–12% whilst enhancing customer service.

There are c5 million LCV/HGV vehicles on the road in Briton[1] (4.5 million LCV and c0.5 million HGV) with the sector employing in excess of five million workers (c16% of UK workforce). The numbers of vehicles procured, and drivers employed, continues to grow annually and in excess of 90% of all goods moved in the UK is via road transportation. Depot-based businesses represent the operating spine of the UK service sector, providing the platform from which these businesses keep Britain's goods, products, installations, and services moving. The need for businesses to be increasingly more productive and efficient is unrelenting; post Brexit, Covid, continuing climate-change challenges, the emerging migration towards electric or hydrogen vehicles, the Ukraine conflict, and with minimum wage momentum ever upwards, the demand on operational managers to achieve more with less has arguably never been greater.

The techniques discussed in each chapter are straightforward to understand, uncomplicated, and can be applied operationally individually and independent of other chapters, alternatively these guideline principles may be consolidated to form a holistic logistics management operating model.

Note

1. Delivering for the Economy. 2019 Report for LCVs. The Society of Motor Manufacturers and Traders Ltd communications@smmt.co.uk. Domestic Road Freight statistics. UK 2019. Lucy Mills. Roadfreight.stats@dft.gov.uk.

Acknowledgements

A personal thank you to those colleagues that have provided an endorsement – your validation and support is hugely appreciated – and to the hundreds of operational managers that I have had the pleasure of working with during the last twenty years and without whose contribution, creativity, and diligence in helping formulate and successfully implementing some of the concepts contained herein, this book would not have been possible.

About the Author

Graduating from Cranfield University in 1986 having attained a Master's degree in Transport Studies aged 31, Colin secured his first management role as "Shift Manager" in 3PL logistics. During the next 14 years, he "learned his trade" in warehousing and distribution in several 3PL companies as Depot then Regional Manager, to be appointed as Regional Operations Manager with Securicor before being offered his first MD role in 2000 with SDS, a privately owned security logistics services company. The business turnaround from loss-making to profit encompassed 200% revenue growth, the business was successfully sold, and Colin joined G4s (CIT Logistics) as the UK Operations director in 2004 with responsibility for c8,500 employees and a fleet of 2,200 specialist vehicles. The 14 years at G4s included two overseas business turnarounds as MD, culminating in being appointed Global Head of Cash logistics in 2012 providing operational support to 56 cash logistics businesses. Appointed COO in 2016 at VPS (Vacant Property Services), he was part of the turnaround team integrating two businesses and achieving best-in-class service before moving to PHS (Hygiene and Waste Services) in 2018 as COO to lead the operational turnaround of the business as part of the Executive team; the business was successfully sold in the summer of 2020 for £495 million to Bidvest. Colin semi-retired in the summer of 2021 to focus on authoring this book, but continues to provide logistics consultancy services to route-based service-sector business.

Chapter 1

People Management

Introduction

Businesses with a depot infrastructure operating commercial fleets will employ the majority of all colleagues at depot, and these colleagues will be broadly split into two groups, warehouse and or store employees who are static and work to structured shift patterns in depot and drivers who operate the commercial vehicle fleet from the depot and who service customers on location, this latter community is essentially a mobile workforce requiring specific management techniques. The number and role of static "warehouse" employees is a function of the volume and complexity of the product stored and the frequency with which the fleet and external suppliers require loading and unloading. There are many publications that focus specifically on warehousing operations; this book is entirely dedicated to fleet and driver management, with guideline techniques on how best to manage both in order to optimise customer service and driver productivity.

Irrespective of the service performed, these are essentially people-based businesses, the organisation may procure sophisticated expensive fleet and may be technically advanced, but its direct workforce (drivers and warehouse) is very likely to reflect its highest single cost, constitute the majority of company employees, and arguably represent the organisation's greatest asset. In some businesses, for example retailers which operate large regional distribution centres (RDCs) 24/7, warehousing employees are likely to reflect the majority of direct (employees that touch the product) colleagues, but in many service companies (especially those operating LCV fleets) the commercial driver community may constitute upwards of 80% of all business employees. This cadre are the face of the organisation that the customer sees and interacts with daily, they deliver the core service reflecting the company's "reason for being," and they operate the commercial vehicle fleet, which is likely to represent the organisation's second highest cost.

The driver community is the heart of the business; manage this cadre effectively, nurture and support them, and this collective will provide a robust service platform that will deliver on the business's contractual obligation, enhance business reputation, and operate at a cost commensurate with business gross margin expectation. Conversely, a poorly managed driver community operating within loosely defined management structures and processes is likely to underperform, underdeliver, and increase operating costs which in turn will dilute the gross margin.

This book provides tips and good-practice guidelines to aid managers to better deliver positive operational results for the company. These techniques have nothing to do with "big-brother" or "micromanaging" employees, but everything to do with communication, continual improvement, and defining operating techniques founded on a platform of robust data that enables pertinent decision making that will aid, not hinder, all operational colleagues to efficiently deliver the service goals that customers expect, deserve, and which they pay for, and this revenue ultimately funds the salaries of both managers and colleagues delivering the service.

Guideline Management Principles

There is a long list of duties, responsibilities, and tasks associated with the role of depot manager (DM), irrespective of the service delivered, it is a multifaceted general management role, and when you strip the component parts down to the core accountabilities, the role is fundamentally one of leadership; route-based organisations are people businesses and the depot manager's role is essentially one of people management; if this core discipline is performed well, all other depot processes and tasks fall into place. Of course there are a host of administrative chores, route planning to oversee, the building and vehicle fleet to maintain, a plethora of company procedures to follow and customer demands to satisfy, day after day, but enabling all of these responsibilities are the people working at the depot, and if the depot manager has the requisite people skills that will bring colleagues together in a positive collaborative way, focused on collectively delivering service to customers, with panache and the ability to overcome the inevitable obstacles they will face each day, colleagues will work with heads up, not down and deliver on customer goals. The DM role is essentially one of leadership, not administration, being accountable for decision making, and being account-able to the colleagues that report and work for you, and look to you for direction, and support.

Depot based colleagues report directly to local depot management, with whom they interact with on a daily basis and look to for reassurance and assistance, these colleagues are most likely to form their view and judgement of the company on the basis and quality of these daily interactions, and local management appreciate the importance of this dynamic and embrace, not recoil from the accountability they have for managing their operational colleagues; it is a fundamental "reason for being" for a depot manager and his or her local management team. The HR department is a *support* func-tion, often with a small team centrally based, albeit some organisations may have a limited regional HR presence, often a single individual covering a large geographical area to umbrella several depot teams. The daily interface between depot management and colleagues will naturally encompass all things welfare, equipment, fleet, PPE, operational performance, productivity, and training, the sparce interactions a driving colleague is likely to have with a dedicated HR colleague or other "non-depot" member of management is likely to reflect less than 2% of all colleague to management interfaces.

All businesses issue a contract of employment to each employee upon commencement with the company and this document may be supplemented with an "Employee Handbook" which together, outlines the employee's rules of engagement and contractual "terms and conditions," with the Handbook incorporating day-to-day core operating procedures. These documents will be periodically updated by the company to reflect current processes and procedures. Additionally, standard operating procedures (SOPs) may supple-ment the Handbook with more detailed instructions; the SOP format is a crisp and precise reference document (often just one or two pages), using photographs or pictures, written in simple language, describing practically how to perform a specific task. SOPs are located at the place of work where the associated task is performed. Whilst the company produces these vari-ous documents, any initial query that a colleague may have is most likely to be raised and dealt with in the first instance by the local depot management team.

The criticality of the DM and his or her direct team regarding colleague interaction cannot be overstated, the company requires and relies almost entirely on the local management team regarding colleague communication and welfare, and at all times to remain professional, even-handed but resolute in promoting and maintaining company policies and procedures with the aim of upholding the highest quality standard of work and customer service; any lapse in management focus and or loosening of these standards is likely to result in similar lapses in colleague behaviour and this dilution will ultimately erode customer quality and service.

Companies produce a contract of employment, policies and procedures, and associated SOPs in order to promote and define the customer service offering together with a detailed methodology of how the service is to be delivered and to what quality standard. Local depot management teams ensure that they, and their depot colleagues, comply with and adhere to these policies and procedures. Being cognisant of the four guideline principles below will help depot teams maintain high quality customer service.

1. *Avoid setting new precedents or deviate from company policy*
   Common examples of setting new precedents or "bending" a procedure might include a relaxation of company holiday rules, non-adherence to conducting absence Return-to-Work (RTW) procedures, knowingly paying incorrect (higher) overtime rates as a "quick fix" to incentivise employees to work extra hours or to complete an urgent customer delivery. The list is endless. It is important that local depot management prevent procedural "creep" and appreciate that initiating new local precedents undermine business objectives and will ultimately reduce depot efficiency, increase costs, and erode management credibility, the DM and team will be judged by depot colleagues in no small part, by the consistency of their decision making and perceived "fairness" of the treatment to themselves comparative to fellow colleagues. It is virtually impossible to keep a management "favour" or procedural indiscretion a "secret," or for a favour "never to be repeated" or a one-off; colleagues will readily inform other colleagues of any management indiscretion, and once a new precedent has been established, no matter how small, it is challenging for local management to take a backward step, they may become a victim of embarrassment or, at worst, concerned that their personal lapse might be discovered by management that reside beyond the depot boundary. Within a matter of a few months of minor indiscretions and "tweaking" of company policy, the depot's procedural foundation can become littered with corrosive precedents.
   Note: Where new precedents have been introduced independently by a DM (unwittingly or otherwise) but remain undetected by senior

management, the arrival of either a new depot manager or 2IC (post a member of the depot team leaving the business) may provide a genuine opportunity to right the "wrong-doing" of previous management once the policy breaches have been discovered and escalated. The "new-broom-sweeps-clean" concept invariably works if the change (in this case company procedures being re-established at the depot) is implemented immediately upon discovery and with requisite HR support; after all, the new manager is simply applying the company rules and or guidelines as per contract and Handbook, and which are being common across the rest of the depot network. If the incumbent DM is in-post at the time non-compliances are discovered, the easiness or otherwise of re-setting company policies and procedures will be linked to the immediacy and robustness with which the DM's indiscretion(s) are dealt with by the company.

2. *Messaging*
Overt messaging

Every interaction, no matter how trivial the content, between a member of management and work colleague is pertinent and should be perceived by management as essentially a "selling" opportunity. The company Sales team "sell" ideas, concepts, and products to customers to persuade them to purchase; operational managers "sell" good practice, reinforcing the need to comply with company policies and procedures (which are designed to deliver requisite service and profitability). The quickest method of instruction is simply to "tell" a colleague to do something, but unless necessary time is taken to explain the "why" and the "how," the colleague is less likely to execute the task diligently and with positivity. Each and every colleague interaction reinforces either positive or negative behaviour. It should not need to be stated, but regrettably experience suggests otherwise, all management communication with a colleague must be delivered without swearing, cursing, or with a raised voice, without inuendo, and always in a respectful and polite tone, one human being to another. Colleagues interact with their fellow colleagues everyday both in and out of work, they will talk to each other about management whether managers like this fact or not. Learned behaviour (good or bad) and tales of management attitude is shared and transmitted across the driver community and woven into the collcagues' communications web is management's "reputation" as perceived by colleagues. Once woven, it is virtually impossible to completely unravel negative perceptions. The tone, mannerism, and clarity of delivery by the manager merge to form the quality of the message being received and will directly influence the quality of output thereafter. Each interaction well "sold," is an opportunity to promote business protocols and demonstrate good leadership, conversely an interaction flippantly or carelessly delivered, in a terse or unprofessional manner, will demotivate the recipient and is likely to result in sub-standard output.

What a manager says, and the manner in which it is said, reflects in the recipient's mind, the inherent values of the business (not only the manager), the local manager, and business are essentially one and the same entity. The business recruited and trained the manager, it is entirely conceivable therefore that he or she is perceived as a business advocate and mouthpiece. A colleague working at a depot interacts directly with members of local management for c98% of all colleague to management transactions, and whilst the business may disseminate all manner of corporate messaging via various other mediums (newsletters, noticeboards, company videos, company literature, etc.) that promote business values and its vision, a colleague is most likely to determine a personal view of the business from his or her experience and dealings with management at the local level.

Sublime messaging

Sublime messaging is subtlety nuanced and managers need to appreciate that saying nothing on occasion may be perceived as tacit endorsement. Management teams must consciously tackle procedural non-compliance or poor behaviour whenever and wherever it is witnessed or discovered, and resolutely avoid swerving from or failing to deal with any non-compliance, no matter how small, simply because the manager is "busy at the time" or because the interface may prove uncomfortable to conduct. Discovered non-compliance warrants dealing with head-on but tactfully, as failure to immediately address the issue, having discovered the issue, may be perceived by the colleague as management endorsing the poor behaviour or non-compliance. If management are to uphold and improve standards at work, it is fundamental for them not to "look the other way," for example:

■ If a driver fails to notify the depot team of a customer "missed" drop (whatever the reason) whilst the driver is at (or intending to drive by) the customer premises, and if subsequently management fail to discuss the reason for this non-compliance and or "drive-by" during the driver debrief process.

■ If driver debrief is not conducted thoroughly and any driver without 100% route completion fails to be debriefed by a member of management.

■ If an RTW interview is not conducted immediately upon return to the depot and before recommencing duties, or the RTW is not conducted thoroughly or conduction left for the administrator to conduct for expediency because the manager is "too-busy."

■ If, following a vehicle incident/accident, the driver is not returned to the depot and the vehicle thoroughly inspected and the incident investigated via a formal interview by management.

■ If telematics reports are not reviewed daily with driving discrepancies and speeding events discussed directly with the driver during debrief, and no later than 24 working hours of the telematics breach having occurred.

■ If swearing or unacceptable, offensive language (by any colleague) is used in the Operations office and not supressed and dealt with appropriately and immediately.

The list of potential examples could fill several pages, the point worth reiterating is that every time a member of management overlooks an indiscretion or fails to address colleague non-compliance, the message being received "loud and clear" by the colleague is that the non-compliance or poor behaviour is deemed by management to be OK … and each transgression not challenged and corrected, pervades by "creep" a dilution of standards across the depot community.

3. *Recruit the right individual for the role, not the first through the door*
   Logistics businesses are fast-paced environments often with demanding contractual service commitments and unrelenting volume throughput, that combined, generate pressurised work environments for both management and colleagues. A core objective for depot management is to maintain requisite driver establishment (the minimum number of drivers needed to fulfil the planned routes necessary to meet customer volume demand) to ensure and to protect customer service. The need to recruit a consistent stream of new employees is necessary in many service organisations and specifically in the larger conurbations (London, Glasgow, Birmingham, Manchester, Leeds, Bristol, etc.) and in companies where attrition rates are persistently high this need to recruit may be on an every-week basis, and in such circumstances, depot

service to customers may become unreliable due to resource constraints if the establishment level is not maintained, and manager's may feel under pressure to uphold the minimum headcount "at-any-cost," and this pressure may manifest in a lowering of standards regarding candidate calibre and culminate in employing applicants with low suitability. However, such a response is likely to increase not reduce short-term (exit within the initial 12 weeks post commencement) attrition. There are no short-cuts to recruiting calibre candidates, and this phenomenon has been accentuated post Brexit combined with a market environment of sustained low levels of national unemployment. The "revolving-door" recruitment syndrome absorbs more, not less management time to repeatedly interview prospective candidates, and overall depot service and costs are likely to worsen as training costs rise, vehicle accidents rise, attrition trends rise not fall, and ultimately service failures (missed services) increase in tandem with service complaints. In severe cases, depots operating in this recruitment cauldron and operating persistent under establishment of drivers can experience a collapse in service operationally within a period of two to three months. Mitigation is best addressed through adequately resourcing the head office and depot recruitment teams (application sifting, interviewing, and vetting) and in depots hardest hit bolster the depot team short term using support (management colleagues) from neighbouring depots to bolster interviewing and support induction, until driver establishment equilibrium is achieved, but critically, do not lower applicant standards and appoint unsuitable, low-calibre candidates as this tactic is likely to perpetuate, not resolve the establishment shortfall.

4. *The root cause of a driver related issue is most likely to rest with management not colleague*
   People come to work to earn money, provide for their family, and forge a career if the opportunity arises. In the main, people are decent, honest folk that work diligently and want to be content when at work and recognised when they do their job well; every colleague, no matter their role, is integral to the business otherwise the role would not exist. The vast proportion of colleagues do not come to work with the aim of being disruptive or fail in their role; therefore, if there is a perceived problem with a colleague or their resulting output, appreciate that the root cause is most likely to be management related not colleague related, with the problem likely to emanate from inadequate training,

an operational process flaw, an absence or lack of clarity regarding the work instruction, inadequate equipment or PPE, or indeed a flawed recruitment process that placed a candidate in a role for which he or she do not possess the requisite core skills.

There will be a tiny minority of colleagues that the above statement does not encapsulate, and who may be deliberately belligerent or disruptive, but it is important to maintain perspective and not to let the discomfort and angst experienced when dealing with this minority unduly influence your demeanour when dealing with the vast body of decent folk who, like you, are getting through each day the best way they can before returning to their family. Decent people deserve being treated decently and will respond in kind to the benefit of the depot.

Two important people management disciplines that directly impact driver availability, aid the establishment level, and influence operating cost are holiday planning and absence management. Having a structured formal process (where none exists) and that is uniformly deployed across all depots applying common metrics and procedures will reduce incidences of absence and will reduce the number of agency staff-days purchased and additionally will decrease overtime trends where a lack of holiday planning has resulted in spiking of employee leave, often during the summer holiday period or during the final month(s) at the end of the holiday calendar year due to log jamming.

Managing Holiday Planning

At least 10% of a colleagues' paid calendar year is consumed by holidays (20 days minimum plus statutory eight bank holidays); with long service and individual company terms, this percentage may exceed 12%+. This percentage reflects a sizeable proportion of the working year, and as every employee enjoys the same benefit, if holidays are not planned effectively by management the negative impact to the business may manifest in reduced customer service and increase costs due to either the recruitment of additional temporary/agency staff and or higher overtime to supplement a temporary establishment gap (number of available drivers at work) due to holiday spiking. Temporary staff are often more expensive than PAYE colleagues, potentially less dependable, and certainly not as well versed or experienced in fulfilling the required role; additionally, they will be less conversant than permanent employees with driving and operating company commercial vehicle which may result in increased vehicle accidents. Implementing a formal holiday process for all operational staff (direct and indirect) is therefore a fundamental requirement for Operations management.

The holiday year starts and ends at various times depending on the company calendar, with the most common start date 1st of April (in line with the new tax year) ending 31st of March. All worked examples in this chapter apply this assumption.

The aims of the holiday process are

1. To ensure that all employee holidays are taken by all colleagues by the holiday "year-end." Colleagues are entitled to and should take their full holiday entitlement for their own well-being, and management should ensure that the business fulfils its duty of care to its employees to achieve this outcome.
2. To "smooth" holiday days taken each month as far as is practical to minimise the need for either overtime (OT) working or supplementary temporary or agency.
3. To take account of predictable business volume including seasonal spikes, and to provide a mechanism to cope effectively with fluctuations via the implementation of an employee "min/max" holiday capacity model.

Good practice principles to include

1. Implement a "first-come-first-serve" booking process locally at each depot, but common in methodology across all depots, to encourage colleagues to actively plan and book their leave. For best results, apply strict formal criteria regarding timelines to request and authorise (including any declined applications) in order to avoid colleague confusion or disagreement between multiple colleagues who apply simultaneously and who may "compete" for similar holiday dates. This process is to encompass the following guidelines:
   a. That a request for leave should be submitted to management by the colleague in writing using a company form (hard or soft copy) and this document will contain the date of submission, the dates requested for leave, and local management will countersign the

request document in order to ensure that both parties have a formal copy of the request, this is useful in the event that a subsequent query arise.

b. The management team should authorise or decline the request within a set period of time (recommended not longer than 48 working hours, excluding weekends, from receipt) from the date of submission. Stretching this timeline increases the likelihood of competing requests and arising disputes, especially during peak holiday periods.

c. Local management create and maintain a large visual, easy-read holiday board at the depot for all employees to view and have easy access to, and this holiday "noticeboard" must be kept updated by the local management team at least twice-weekly to ensure the data therein remains "current." This board should display, for every employee, the number of holiday days/weeks booked (by individual by week) and taken, and the number of remaining "available" days outstanding but not yet requested.

2. For recognised peak holiday periods that attract a high percentage of colleague requests (i.e., Christmas, summer school holiday period, Easter, and other religious occasions) and which may not be able to be fully satisfied due to high demand, management will ensure that a strict roster system, that is fair and transparent, is implemented so that colleagues not allocated a peak holiday request (for example Christmas) one year are prioritised the following year. This rotational method must be seen to be equitable.

3. Avoid colleague favouritism when authorising holiday requests and refrain from including additional selection criteria (i.e., length of service) that may be perceived as disadvantaging sections of the employee base.

4. Apply a maximum and minimum limit (%) regarding the number of colleagues permitted to be granted leave in any department or cadre in any one week. For example, in a business without volume peaks or troughs and assuming the majority of colleagues enjoy 20 or 21 holidays annually plus bank holidays, the recommended min–max levels might be:

Maximum 10% (a depot of 50 drivers the maximum would be five)
Minimum 8% (in the same depot the minimum target is four)

The minimum target level should be as close to the maximum (in this example 10%) level as is practical for management to achieve every week. From the commencement of the new holiday year programme, every week that passes where the actual number taking holiday falls below the "minimum" target will in practice mean that the minimum level will need adjustment (upwards) to compensate in future months in order to claw back any negative variance by year end, and thereby avoid a log jam scenario. However, providing the gap between the accumulative minimum and base plan remains relatively small, then employee attrition (the number of employees that leave the business each month) may partially compensate for the shortfall as some of these leavers will have outstanding holidays not taken at the time of their exit, and new starters are less likely to request holidays during their induction period unless pre-arranged.

5. Holidays not taken (outstanding) should not be permitted to be "carried-forward" into the following holiday year and neither should this residue holiday be paid in-lieu. Residue days need to be forfeit (based on a "use it or lose it" basis) to encourage appropriate colleague behaviour throughout the year; both the employee and company have a responsibility to ensure that holiday entitlement is fully used. Exceptional and unforeseen circumstances (e.g. where illness or family tragedy impacts leave during the last few weeks of the holiday year) can be dealt with sensitively and treated as a special case, with senior management's discretion if warranted. Where the employee contract does not reflect a "use it or lose it" policy it is recommended that HR should collaborate with colleagues and management to revise the terms and conditions accordingly. The primary aim (as stated above) is for all holidays to be taken in full, the inclusion of a perceived "escape clause" may disincentivise some colleagues from actively booking leave; however, experience suggests that such incidences are uncommon and result usually from poor individual holiday planning (which this process will address with diligent management) rather than a desire not to take full advantage of holiday entitlement.

6. The business might also consider segmenting the calendar year and stipulating the minimum number of holiday days (excluding bank holidays) that are to be taken in each segment, this structure aids "smoothing" of holidays to avoid spiking and helps sharpen the focus of the employee to be cognisant of booking leave in the near future rather than solely considering the main family annual holiday. In the example below, the holiday calendar is April to March but incorporates a "redringed" (zero holiday policy and contractual commitment) period to help maximise staff attendance and customer service stability during

the known peak trading period. If the annual contractual holidays (excluding bank holidays) is within a range of 21–24, it is recommended that 1–4 days are recognised and able to be retained as "floating" and can be taken at short notice at any time to support those unforeseen life events that everyone experiences on occasion, for example a sudden family or friend's death, a child's birth, the emergency dental visit, etc. In Figure 1.1, the annual holiday entitlement is 21 days excluding bank holidays. More days can be authorised and taken beyond the minimum, for example a colleague may take two weeks (ten days) in June, in which case the colleague is comfortably ahead of the minimum target, this is to be encouraged where feasible, and in such circumstances, management should view the minimum target as incremental, five by June, ten by September as a minimum and so on.

7. When calculating the maximum percentage, round-up not "down" and plan using full not part heads. For example, if 87 drivers of similar skill set work at a particular depot then a maximum of 10% reflects 8.7 heads so round-up to nine when target setting.

8. Holidays are important to all employees and may become a point of contention if a request for leave is declined for any reason, so the management team need to be diligent in administering the process and adhere to the agreed processing timelines to be seen to be equitable in decision making. The holiday booking process needs to be transparent and explained to new recruits at the interview stage not post-commencement. If a request is to be declined, then explain the decision on a face-to-face basis (e.g. at debrief) not via text and demonstrate the mechanics of the decision (for example there was only one remaining holiday in a given week and colleague X submitted his request a day before colleague Y) but importantly do discuss with the colleague alternative availability in order to try to bring about a positive resolution. New starters with pre-booked holidays (organised before the interview

April – June	5 days
July – September	5 days
October – December (excluding Dec)	3 days
January – March	5 days
Total minimum	18 days (allowing 3 floating)

Figure 1.1 Example of minimum holiday segmentation by quarter assuming 21 base holidays per annum excluding bank holidays.

date) should have these holidays honoured but these days need not form part of the base holiday min–max plan and disadvantage existing employees.

9. This process requires regular communication and a current holiday board so that colleagues have full transparency. Colleagues must not be disciplined for being tardy regarding their holiday planning, it is management's responsibility to fully understand the current and future holiday situation including an appreciation of the individuals that are lagging behind, and it is for management to own the challenge to prompt colleagues to book and take leave. To this end, depot management should formally review the colleague holiday position vs. plan at least weekly.

Having a formal depot annual plan (Figure 1.2) at the start of the year and subsequently measuring progress against the plan is a fundamental requirement. The example plan assumes an establishment of 87 drivers with the holiday year running between April and March. Zero holidays are permitted to be taken during November and December as this period reflects the business peak.

Without a formal process, a depot management team may fail to achieve the targeted outcome. A depot plan must be updated at least weekly and be reviewed by senior line management (regional or national operations manager) at least monthly.

It is useful if the "variance to plan" line is RAG (red, amber, green) coloured to provide an "easy-read" indication of performance at a glance. In Figure 1.2, if the variance to plan is less than a one-colleague holiday week (five holiday days), the RAG status is "green," if six to nine days amber, and ten days (two employee weeks equivalent) or greater the status indicates "red."

There will be multiple reasons why the actual results may not exactly meet plan, for example a new starter may have pre-booked holiday, an employee may have an unexpected "life event" requiring urgent leave. Trend performance is more meaningful than a weekly "snapshot" and having a periodic review of performance (actual vs. plan) enables local management together with the reviewing line manager to understand the root causes, and in instances where actual is adrift from plan, mutually agree requisite corrective actions whilst simultaneously adjusting future target setting in order to arrest any current shortfall in order to achieve the year-end target. Regarding the plan, the closer a future week is to the current week the higher the expectation would be for

Months	April				May					June				July				August				September				
Weeks	1	2	3	4	5	6	7	8	9	10	11	12	13	14	15	16	17	18	19	20	21	22	23	24	25	26
Plan days	35	35	35	35	45	45	45	45	45	45	45	45	45	45	45	45	45	45	45	45	45	40	40	40	40	40
Plan heads	7	7	7	7	9	9	9	9	9	9	9	9	9	9	9	9	9	9	9	9	9	8	8	8	8	8
Actual days	34	30	35	35	40	46	48	45	46	45	47	45	48	45	45	46										
Variance	-1	-6	-6	-6	-11	-10	-7	-7	-6	-6	-4	-4	-1	-1	-1	0										
Booked																	46	45	42	46	46	45	41	38	35	35
Accum variance																	1	1	-2	-1	0	0	1	-1	-6	-11

Months	October				November				December					January				February				March				
Weeks	27	28	29	30	31	32	33	34	35	36	37	38	39	40	41	42	43	44	45	46	47	48	49	50	51	52
Plan days	35	35	35	40										40	35	35	35	35	35	35	35	40	40	40	40	40
Plan heads	7	7	7	8										8	7	7	7	7	7	7	7	8	8	8	8	8
Actual days																										
Variance																										
Booked	30	20	20	15										5	0	0	0	0	10	0	0	0	5	0	20	0
Accum variance	-16	-31	-45	-80																						

Note: "Zero holidays" across November–December.

Figure 1.2   An example annual holiday planner for 87 drivers with an easy-read RAG status.

the status to be "green," in Figure 1.2 for the whole month of October (three months hence from current date – which is indicated by the vertical black arrow) all weeks are "red" RAGGED and requiring local management to actively review which colleagues need "targeting" to encourage them to book holidays.

10. Within each depot the holiday planning board must display the 52 weeks of the holiday year and include a dedicated "row" for each individual colleague and within this colleague row have sufficient granularity that each week has five individual cells representing a single day's holiday. A colleague should be able to look at the board and immediately identify his or her holiday status regarding the number of holiday days taken (to the individual day, not week), the number and which days/weeks are future booked (but not yet taken), and the number of days that remain outstanding (available but not yet booked). Each colleague should have a current RAG indicator cell so at a glance he or she can appreciate if they are currently "on-track" with their holiday planning or need to be more urgently considering their next period of leave.

Sickness and Absence Management

A creditable absence performance for a business at the national and individual depot level reflects a consistent overall percentage of sub-3% whether the business is unionised or not, and this percentage figure reflects the consolidated position including all sickness categories (short and long term) and all absence categories but excludes holiday leave. Management should share the sub-3% aspiration with colleagues, it is not a clandestine objective but an overt and entirely reasonable goal. In 2020, UK average overall sickness and absence fell to a new low level of 1.8% with Covid representing 14% of all sickness[1]; since 2000, the average rate has been maintained at sub-3%, with the "Transport" and or "Distribution" sector statistics reflecting a "mid-table" position relative to other sectors. The most common sub-category for illness is classified as "minor illness" including coughs, colds, flu, nausea, and diarrhoea.

The absence percentage is measured by calculating the total number of sick and absent hours (by department, depot, and nationally) in a given period (week or financial accounting period) over the total number of employee (excluding holiday) paid and unpaid combined hours on the payroll for the period.

Figure 1.3 provides an example applying the 87-driver establishment number, with two vacancies and categorisation of those not at work for a sample period of one week:

The overall absence percentage for this sample week is outlined in Figure 1.4.

Including holiday hours would artificially decrease the absence rate by adding more hours into the total hours "pot" but colleagues on leave are not planned to be at work, in the example above the percentage would fall to 2.3% (when rounded up) if holiday hours were encompassed.

Experience suggests that the vast majority employees naturally present low (sub-3%) absence consistently, with poor absence rates expressed in a low proportion of the employee base (–10%). Maintaining meticulous data records at the individual colleague level in order to provide management with accurate absence trends by both the employee and across a cadre is a fundamental requirement in order to understand, monitor, and better control absence.

Genuine illness can impact anyone in society at any time for a multitude of reasons and management need to be supportive in instances of genuine sickness. The most effective methodology to improving absence rates is to address the minority of colleagues that demonstrate short-term (1–3 days) persistent and repeated absence/sickness incidences. The Bradford[2] Factor scoring methodology is not recommended as a mechanism to monitor and control sickness as short-term absence attracts disproportionately low scores which can mask poor underlying trends.

Driver establishment	87
Number of vacancies	2
Holiday weeks (full week equivalent)	8
Absence (unpaid) 5 days	1
Short-term sickness (paid) 5 days	1
Long-term sickness	0
Drivers working	75

Figure 1.3   Example classification of 87 drivers' activities for a one-week period.

Drivers @ work contract hours (75*40)	3,000
15 of the 75 complete OT hours	175
320 holiday hours used	0
Absence (unpaid) 5 days	(40)
Short-term sickness (paid) 5 days	(40)
Long-term sickness	0
Absence % = 80 / 3,175	**2.5%**

Figure 1.4   Example calculation of the absence percentage based on the activity classification in Figure 1.3.

In similar fashion to monitoring holidays, a detailed record for every employee must be maintained and incorporate an easy-read visual schematic (used for management purposes) which can be used to illustrate an individual's record and demonstrate how an individual's trend compares to depot colleagues from within the same cadre. An example can be seen in Figure 1.5. If company IT systems cannot readily produce a similar data model automatically, then it is incumbent on the local operational management team to create this tool "long-hand"; the author has introduced Excel versions nationwide in several companies and in depots with one hundred plus drivers. In businesses with multiple locations, senior management should ensure that templates are common to enable comparative analysis between depots. Where local management teams have not used this method of analysis previously, there may be pockets of initial resistance, often on the basis that "it absorbs too much management time," but the benefits to the local team and to the business overall far outweigh the minor daily task (10–20 minutes for an administrator depending on driver numbers to update an Excel sheet) of updating straightforward attendance records, and deployment of such a tool will aid reduction in absence in just a few months post introduction. For best results, the tool is used in conjunction with conducting formal Return-to-Work (RTW) interviews and implementing targeted formal absence reviews for repeat "offenders" and, over time, as absence improves so will the net (colleagues at work) establishment number which will in turn aid customer service and reduce overall labour costs.

Week	Week 1					Week 2					Week 3					Week 4				
Day	M	Tu	W	T	F	M	Tu	W	T	F	M	Tu	W	T	F	M	Tu	W	T	F
Colleague 1						LT	LT	LT	LT	LT	LT	LT	LT	LT	LT					
Colleague 2				A																
Colleague 3	ST											ST				ST				
Colleague 4																				
Colleague 5			IAW																	

Weeks	1	2	3	4	5	6	7	8	9	10	11	12	13	Total	%	FY	%
Colleague 1		5	5											10	15%	12	5%
Colleague 2														0	0%	2	1%
Colleague 3	1		1	1				1					1	5	8%	17	7%
Colleague 4														0	0%	0	1%
Colleague 5	1									1				2	3%	5	2%

A	Absent not sick	ST	Short-term sickness
IAW	Injury whilst at work	LT	Long-term sickness

Figure 1.5   Example of absence tracker by colleague by week, and quarterly trend with full-year (FY) projection assuming trend sustained.

Figure 1.5 illustrates the simplicity of the data requiring daily collation and input into a basic Excel spreadsheet. Employees are sub-divided into compatible work cadres (i.e., Drivers, Warehouse, Administration, etc.) so that when absence trends are reviewed between management and colleague to discuss their absence record, management are seen to be comparing performance on a like-for-like basis with colleagues performing similar roles. It is *not* advisable to overtly publish sickness and absence data sets or pin them to common notice boards as the information may be deemed sensitive personal data, but it is reasonable to show these tables to a colleague during a review (with other colleague's names "hidden" from sight) in order to dem-onstrate their (the individual colleague being reviewed) personal absence record in detail individually and comparatively with other colleagues that work in the depot, and indeed comparatively to the business national aver-age (all depot data) relevant to that particular cadre.

It is also reasonable to RAG the current and accumulative absence record and forecast a year-end position. The RAG in Figure 1.5 indicates the follow-ing ranges:

Green	Sub-3%
Amber	3%–5%
Red	5%+

The majority of colleagues are likely to demonstrate a trend of sub-3% con-sistently. The benefit to management of forecasting the year-end position is that individual colleagues might experience genuine serious illness (i.e., Colleague 1 in Figure 1.5) and may appear to present as having an absence problem when a snapshot view is taken, but when their previous history is considered, and the reason for absence analysed, the longer-term projection is likely to suggest (a) an improving trend and (b) a trend not warranting formal review but rather a "watching brief" to ensure the colleague's welfare is being appropriately supported by management.

Colleague three (Figure 1.5) however is demonstrating a concerning trend in that a Monday appears to present as a root cause for repeated absence, and across the 13-week review, this colleague has taken five individual one-day absences. Single-day absence, and specifically same-day absences may reflect causation that is not illness related. If the RTW process is applied diligently, then post the second one-day incident the root cause will hope-fully be identified and addressed, with three single-day or three absence incidences within a 13-week period reflecting a trend prompting in all reasonableness, a trigger to commence a formal disciplinary and corrective process.

One-day absence is particularly disruptive operationally and customer service is likely to be impacted because it is unplanned, possibly unannounced (until the morning of the absence) with the fallout including planned work (driver routes) for customers terminated resulting in lost business revenue and a tarnished service performance. The wider driver colleague community at the depot recognise other persistent offenders, indeed they may be requested to work OT to compensate for another colleague's absence, and or requested to adopt some of the "lost" services resulting from their colleague's unplanned absence causing them personal disruption. The depot's "silent majority" will monitor management's response to chronic "offenders" with interest and quietly understand what remedial action, if any, management take. If persistent absence in other individuals is not addressed, it may encourage "copycat" behaviour in fellow colleagues, the "sublime message" is that management accept or endorse the behaviour and high absence, and this will erode the credibility of local management, undermine depot performance, and may lower standards in other colleagues.

Once a formal disciplinary process is triggered, it is straightforward for management to progress through the disciplinary phases if the absence trend persists; however, one hopes that early formal intervention will generally prompt the colleague to address the root cause, change patterns of behaviour, and they will set about improving their absence rates to a more normalised level in line with the depot cadre average.

Employee Attrition

Attrition is the number and rate (measured as a percentage) of leavers during each financial accounting period and accumulatively throughout the year. It is often measured using a rolling 12- or 13-month metric together with the last three-month's metric used to gauge both short- and long-term trends. The rate of attrition is an anchor KPI (key performance indicator – see Chapter 8) in any business where attrition is trending at 25% or greater, as this exit rate trend will be directly impacting the cost of operations, and in depots where rates are higher (inner city depots for example), service delivery will be impacted; 25%+ levels will also drain management time as their focus is required disproportionately on interviewing and training tasks, and HR departments will have increased vetting, recruiting, and advertising costs. Attrition is likely to be nuanced with rural depots less impacted, but in high colleague "turnover" geographies (most likely London, the South-East, and other major large conurbations) attrition may drive the need to recruit literally on a weekly basis.

Studies estimating the genuine cost of recruiting an employee vary significantly. This cost is in part linked to the size of the business, and whether the business has its own HR department or whether the company is dependent on external suppliers for support. The cost associated with recruiting direct (those employees, including drivers, that "touch" the product) staff is estimated to be in the range of £2,500–£3,500 encompassing an average time of four to five weeks representing induction and training. This cost does not include any lost revenue and or credits paid to customers due to missed services resulting from having insufficient drivers.

There are many reasons why employees leave a business including

1. Betterment (educational or to enhance their career path). If the current business does not provide opportunity for career progression.
2. Financial reward. It is not uncommon for LCV drivers for example to be borderline minimum wage earners and therefore more likely to leave the business to do the same type of work for small increases in the hourly rate, or where additional bonus or other "soft" benefits apply. Businesses that provide an opportunity for colleagues to work overtime (OT) may also be more attractive to employees that are willing to work longer than the standard contracted hours.
3. Fundamental working conditions. For example, moving away from weekend working or evening/night shift working.
4. Personal reasons. Family or life incidents which may prompt the need for change, for example having a baby or serious illness in a close relative who may need additional care.
5. Health reasons. Serious personal illness or some other ailment which prevents the employee from being physically able to perform his or her duties safely.
6. Retirement.
7. Proximity to home. A similar job or a similar paid role that is closer to home means more time at home and less personal travel time and associated costs. If a family change their place of residence, they may need to change their place of work.

8. Dismissal. For either gross misconduct or via a succession of performance failings over time.
9. The job role itself, including:
   a. A lack of skills or ability/compatibility to do the work to the minimum required standard
   b. Lack of training or inadequate training
   c. Perceived or actual poor management culture
   d. Lack of equipment or processes and or equipment that is not user-friendly or easy to learn and use
   e. Lack of PPE or inadequate PPE
   f. An inability to cope with size of the vehicle or required vehicle manoeuvres (lots of reversing into tight spaces)
   g. The role is perceived as physically too demanding

The "Reason for Leaving" matrix (Figure 1.6) categorises the reasons by the level of control and influence that management teams can wholly or partially exert. Whilst addressing particular reasons (e.g. 2. Financial reward) may come at a price to the business, if for example the pay rate was increased in a specific geography to stem attrition and attract new recruits for a niche skillset that is critical to delivering customer service, the additional cost may prove less than the reputational impact and supplementary costs (overtime, agency heads, missed service credits, etc.) that the business is burdened with to maintain service.

No.	Description	Full management control	Partial management control	No management control
1	Betterment		✓	
2	Financial Reward		✓	
3	Fundamental working conditions	✓		
4	Personal reasons			✓
5	Health			✓
6	Retirement			✓
7	Proximity to home			✓
8	Dismissal		✓	
9	The job itself			
9.1	Lack of skills, compatibility, suitability		✓	
9.2	Lack of or inadequate training / induction	✓		
9.3	Management culture	✓		
9.4	Equipment, inadequate or insufficient	✓		
9.5	Lack of or suitability of PPE	✓		
9.6	Driving skills related to company LCV/HGV		✓	
9.7	The role is physically too demanding			✓

Figure 1.6 Employee "reason for leaving" matrix.

It is beneficial that the HR team conduct an "exit interview" with each employee that leaves the business (unless dismissed) to understand in detail, independent of operations, and from the colleague's perspective the reasons why the employee decided to leave the business. The interview need not be face-to-face as this adds unnecessary cost and management time and may not be practical in a multi-depot business. The benefits of exit interviews include:

- An independent (not exclusively line-management feedback) assessment of the reasons for leaving.
- A central business repository which leaver data can be channelled through, collated, and from which monthly trend statistics published.
- A developing understanding of trends including the nuanced reasons at individual depot, regional, and national levels.
- Early indication (red flag) of genuine examples of poor management behaviour emerging at a particular depot, such feedback is less likely to arise naturally via local management feedback, but HR exit interviews may identify trends which may otherwise remain undetected.
- Understanding if local competitors or other influences are causing a drain of resource in a specific geography and whether the root cause is driven primarily by earnings or other incentives, and this feedback may enable management to construct a counter strategy to arrest specific driver migration.

Partial Management Control

Betterment

If the colleague is changing the career direction or moving to a new business sector, there may be little the business can do to prevent change; however, if the colleague is migrating to a competitor and is a valued colleague with potential career development, the business may consider incentives to help retain the colleague, and these do not have to be remunerative, the prospect of training and genuine role development can motivate.

Fundamental Working Conditions

If an employee is leaving because the job is fundamentally not what they are seeking (i.e., shift working, weekend working, fixed start time, or end times that conflict with the "school-run," etc.), the business will have little influence, but management should revisit (if the employee has less than one year's service) the recruitment process locally and or at the head office to resolve the question as to why the employee was offered a role initially when the candidate's suitability has proven to be so at odds with the business environment, could and should this disconnect have been teased out during the interview stages, does the recruitment process need finessing?

Dismissal

A gross misconduct offence is likely to be the responsibility of the individual; however, other dismissals may reflect the culmination of a three- to five-stage process which may have taken several months before ending in dismissal. Whilst management should not lower expectation of a colleague's standards of behaviour or work performance, and a small minority of colleagues may reflect a "lost-cause"; nonetheless, managers need to be cognisant that the primary aim of the staged disciplinary process is to correct and improve colleague behaviour and performance. Do not lose faith in a colleague until they have lost the desire to work for management. Post the initial disciplinary phase, ongoing interactions may be uncomfortable and occasionally combative for either or both parties, but if management remain professionally positive and foster a constructive interface whilst providing requisite support and training to address the root cause that initiated the disciplinary process, the colleague may find a way to reengage with the business and move constructively forward. It is less costly and less time consuming to retain rather than replace a colleague if this outcome is mutually beneficial to both parties.

Full Management Control

Each element in this sub-section requires a business periodic review to analyse comparators to understand if the business is leading or lagging behind competitors in a specific category and consider what, if any, modification to the employee contractual terms and conditions or training programmes might arrest the attrition rate without detriment to profitability.

Financial Reward

LCV direct staff often earn close to the UK minimum wage and therefore are unlikely to remain loyal to a business unless other factors significantly outweigh modest monetary incentive. Drivers may "job-hop" for increases in pay of less than £1.00 (one pound) per hour on the basic rate, and whilst a business has a budget and profit targets to achieve, and any increase in driver pay will negatively impact planned costs; a business must remain competitive in the marketplace regarding its ability to attract and recruit new entrants. To prevent colleague attrition reaching a level that is debilitating to customer service, management may consider the following points:

a. Conduct regular (at least twice per annum) market assessment surveys to gauge wages and benefits to understand where the business is, relative to direct competitors and businesses employing similarly qualified drivers. Market conditions can change quickly, for example if a large corporate opens an NDC/RDC in close proximity to a depot, the local pay-rate equilibrium can be quickly disrupted. Compare overall earnings and not simply the basic hourly rate and include a review of bonuses and other soft incentives.

b. Pay increases do not need to be applied nationally but can be targeted locally to combat higher competitive rates. The more comprehensive the analysis from (a) above the more specific and less costly the solution might be.

c. Offering indirect benefits may prove a differentiator when job seekers compare one business to another:
   i. The ability to take the commercial vehicle home.
   ii. Operate routes on a home-to-home basis and reduce the in-depot visit to once (not twice) each day.
   iii. Death in service insurance. It is low cost to introduce but can provide significant potential benefit to lower-earning families.
   iv. Payments for successful "find a friend" initiatives for new recruits once probation has been successfully achieved.
   v. Supplementary reward schemes that are formal and regularly pay out (quarterly) rather than an annual scheme, having to defer gratification for too long. Such schemes might include rewards for zero absence, minimal speeding events (telematics), or one-off joining bonuses linked to retention.

d. Bonus payments. The caveat with any bonus scheme is that it must provide a genuine win-win to both the business and the employee; once a scheme is introduced, it is challenging to remove and leaves a bitter taste for the colleague for years to come. Any new bonus scheme must be well thought through, be pertinent in five years' time, simple to understand and calculate, and deliver tangible benefit to the company. Focus on attendance (a retention payment) combined with absence and sickness rates sustained over a stated period of time with a minimum target to achieve sub-3%. Consider incentivising accident-free driving or zero "speeding events" if the fleet has telematics. Avoid "productivity" schemes, good management teams will continually seek to improve productivity on an ongoing basis, so avoid establishing a premature or sub-optimal benchmark which ultimately renders business benefit redundant, the bonus is effectively being paid for a target that would have been achieved via introducing Lean or other continuous projects. Rather than "productivity" (e.g. drops per hour) focus on output metrics that do not inhibit continual improvement, for example full route completion of all drops with zero "misses" or partially completed jobs.

e. Consider introducing in-house or sponsored training courses that provide genuine advancement to the colleague, but to ensure the "win-win" element, the business must have a genuine need for and capacity to employee once the individual completes said training (e.g. HGV training). Ensure a contractual "claw back" of training expenses is incorporated to help prevent the employee leaving the business post training. The claw back should be time bound (recommended two years). Whilst such a clause may be difficult to enforce in practice, inclusion is worthwhile and aids retention.

Lack of Skills

If an employee exits the business quickly post commencement due to a lack of skills, the root cause may reflect a flaw in the recruitment process. A robust recruitment process should ensure that each applicant offered a role has the requisite core skills. Understand the minimum role requirements and structure the process to deliver a candidate with requisite skillset, for example introduce simple literacy and numeracy tests (there are several readily available on the market) to ensure the applicant has adequate reading and writing skills, a fundamental requirement when using PDAs/Tablets in their everyday work; and where testing is deployed, ensure such tests are completed in depot to avoid intervention by a third party. Conduct physical passport and driving licence checks (not photocopies) at the first interview stage and verify training certification by viewing original documents or verify via exam bodies. The author has also deployed simple tests to verify candidate personal preferences, for example their attention to detail where accuracy is paramount.

Vetting is important. The process will take time and incur cost but not to verify at least the last place of work to check start/leaving dates and the candidates "reason for leaving" is naïve and sloppy. An absence of a process is decision making founded on chance and will increase the likelihood of early exit. The further back in time and more companies vetted the more reliable the vetting process will be, but there is a trade-off between cost and the time it takes to complete vetting so strike a balance. But as a minimum ensure each candidate completes a comprehensive list of previous companies, reasons for leaving, and start and end dates (to within a month) for every previous position, and where gaps in time appear, explore in depth at interview.

A minority of companies conduct a "trial" day which involves the applicant "doing the job" in a limited way, in tandem with a trainer as part of the recruitment process to provide the candidate a genuine "feel for the job" and what appreciate the tasks the role entails, a by-product is that it enables the depot trainer to assess the applicant's suitability and attitude. Whilst this process may deter some candidates, the calibre of starters is likely to be better, and arguably it is better not to start a low-calibre candidate with low job interest, rather than waste time and money on induction training and issuing new PPE only to "lose" the new recruit in a matter of weeks.

It is also recommended that local management conduct a pseudo driving (vehicle manoeuvres) test within the depot yard (see also Chapter 2 – "Fleet Management") using an established and proven test scenario (designed with the fleet manager's involvement) using cones to avoid damage to the vehicle, that will help tease out the applicant's ability to handle large LCVs or non-standard HGV vehicles. This test must include a reversing element as a significant percentage of commercial vehicle incidents and accidents during the first year in post are likely to involve slow speed reversing maneuverers.

Management Culture

In this context, the phrase reflects feedback of a leaver complaint (acquired during exit interview) concerning the attitude or behaviour of one or more individuals that make up the depot management and administrative team, for example a manager may be accused of demonstrating an uncompromising attitude, swearing, bullying, not treating all employees equitably, or the leaving employee may complain of being pressurised to work by management in a manner which is neither safe nor in line with the business procedure. The view or accusation may be false or true but worthy of knowing and warrants further review. Isolated negative feedback will be difficult to verify and may reflect a disgruntled leaver, but an emerging trend of such complaints from multiple leavers gives credence to the complaint and will warrant formal senior management investigation. If the feedback is accurate and the root cause is not addressed, the depot may have an emerging employee-relations problem, and depot service quality locally may be in decline as a consequence.

Conversely, an operation that is data-led with a fast-paced operating rhythm within which colleagues may operate an array of modern technological devices including PDAs, Tablets, in-cab telematics, and where a formal daily debrief is conducted including KPI reviews, such an environment may initially seem daunting to a driver or a new employee who is not accustomed to working in such structured surroundings and which may initially "look and feel" like Big Brother and overly intrusive.

That said, poor management culture does prevail on occasion and may manifest in a failure of management to uphold day-to-day business protocols (i.e., holiday booking/authorisation process, adequate stock management, tardy replacement of equipment or PPE, failure to deal effectively with pay queries, etc.) all of which, from the colleague's perspective, reflect a lack of care. Unprofessional, rude, and sometimes bullying behaviour is perpetrated occasionally (experience suggests such behavioural incidents are rare) within a depot environment; but with good HR governance incorporating the exit interview process, combined with a company confidential whistleblowing line capability, will help identify emerging trends at an early stage. Another route to discovery is the arrival of a new member of a local depot management team, either transferring from an alternative "in-house" depot or external recruit, he or she may witness unacceptable management behaviour and is either confident in the support of the company, or sufficiently distanced from the existing team dynamic to escalate concerns to senior management.

Driving Skills

The qualified HGV driver has been professionally trained and passed a stringent test and will therefore have a guaranteed minimum standard of skill; however, the novice HGV driver may need additional support and time to develop their recently acquired skills.

This sub-section is most pertinent therefore to LCV (van) drivers. Some LCVs are modified post chassis manufacture for a host of reasons, and as a result, the "standard-van" can become uncommonly large dimensionally, furnished with an array of technological devices, be significantly heavier influencing braking distances, and encompass ancillary equipment which may present genuine handling and learning challenges to driver applicants; it is good practice therefore to:

- Conduct predetermined handling manoeuvres including reversing tests with candidates at the second interview stage; these can be conducted by a member of the Training department, or a trusted colleague who has received requisite training, in the depot yard (which is effectively a private road) using cones.
- During the first month of employment, management should conduct extensive analysis (every working day) of driver behaviour and driving techniques via on-board telematics (which provide current and accurate feedback regarding speeding, braking, and cornering events, and will also notify in real time of collision impact). If poor trends are discovered and the driver does not immediately rectify and improve behaviour, it may be prudent to terminate employment during probation rather than regret not having taken decisive action at a later date.

The Role Is Too Physically Demanding

If the role involves physical lifting, stretching and this is standard practice during a route involving multiple drops and associated stop-starts with incidences of access and egress to the vehicle, or the "on-location" activity requires significant walking, stair-climbing, lifting, and or carrying, then management need to be cognisant of the basic level of fitness required to conduct the role day-in and day-out and ensure that the candidate is fully aware that the job content and appreciate that it is much more than sitting in cab driving for most of the working day. The one-day trial day may also prove useful in this regard.

Return-To-Work (RTW) Interview

The RTW interview is not an administrative task and should not be conducted by an administrative colleague. It is important that local (depot) management take direct accountability for conducting this task, which is a management function, and in doing so, will demonstrate to the recipient the importance of the process. The RTW interview is a formal process that entails every colleague, irrespective of role or length of service, to receive a formal interview on the day that he or she returns from sickness or absence, irrespective of the number of days of absence, with their line manager in order to ensure that they are fit to return to work and to discuss the reasons relating to their absence.

For best results and to give credibility to the process, the RTW must be conducted on the day of the return to work, at the start of the working day (whatever the shift start-time) but before the colleague commences work duties. If the colleague was originally signed-off by a doctor as "unfit to work," the colleague should bring with them a certificate stating "signed-fit" to return to work, if the colleague's General Practitioner (GP) has not signed a certificate declaring the colleague as fit for work, or the manager has no evidence of fitness, the manager might send the colleague home to remain "absent" until the requisite documentation is produced and the colleague formally signed-fit to return. This response is neither rude nor discourteous, it protects the business from a potential future claim, and it avoids the problematic situation if the colleague commences work and subsequently falls sick or has an accident/incident whilst at work before being formally deemed "fit-to-return" by a doctor. This process must be reflected in either the employee contract or Handbook, and if it is not then HR should consider its inclusion.

The primary reason for conducting the RTW is management's duty of care to ensure that employees are safe and fit to perform their duties and this process is the gateway to ensure good governance; and conducting the RTW is as important post a one-day absence as it is following return from prolonged sickness. There must be exclusions or exceptions to this process.

The key to ensure a comprehensive interview (whether RTW, Disciplinary, or Accident investigation) is thorough preplanning and data preparation (see Figure 1.7) by the manager. At the start of day, management is often consumed with a myriad of operational matters geared towards galvanising driving and warehouse colleagues to engage and mobilise the fleet to commence scheduled routes; in this bustling environment, the easy thing to do is to instruct an administrator to conduct a cursory RTW or for the manager to delay the RTW until debrief at shift end. Neither option is appropriate, it may encourage further absence and the "sublime message" is that management either do not have the employee's interests at heart (if

RTW Data preparation	
Employee name & ID number	Role type (Driver, warehouse, etc)
Date sickness / absence commence	Name & address of G.P. Surgery
Last working day prior to sickness / absence	Nature (reason) for absence / sickness
Date of last (previous) absence	Has employee been signed fit to return to work?
Number of days / weeks since last absence	Are all sick certificates signed, and span the absence period?
Date RTW conducted (previous absence)	Are there remaining symptoms or colleague issues
Total days / incidences of absence during the last 12 months	Was medical intervention (e.g. hospital) required

Conducting the RTW
Welcome the colleague back to work
Explain the RTW process and structure and aim of the 1-2-1
What action was taken by the Doctor and or Hospital to address sickness?
Are there residue Hospital visits and or medication required, and why, are there inhibiting factors regarding work?
Are there other issues or conditions or concerns the colleague wishes to bring to management's attention?
Appraise the colleague of his / her previous absence record, and how this compares to other colleagues at depot and nationally

Both Manager & Colleague sign & date the RTW document

Determine outcome & next steps
1. Reviewing evidence and having discussed with the colleague, does the manager perceive the reason for absence as genuine?
2. Is there a clear sickness trend, or is a trend emerging, and is a formal discipline (or continuation of the disciplinary process) warranted, outline the reasons why?
3. Have you discussed and agreed a future corrective action plan with the colleague?
4. Is support or guidance required from HR?
5. Have you updated your line manager?

Figure 1.7   The RTW interview process summarised.

the colleague has been genuinely ill or absent long term) and or that the absence (whatever the root cause might have been) is tacitly endorsed by management, and if the absence was not genuine, this flippant response is likely to perpetuate repeated future instances.

Before the RTW interview begins, management should have collated the following data in readiness and this data collation exercise is best completed at the end of the previous day during a quiet moment if the intent to return is notified, where management have not received notification but are aware of potential impending return, data is best prepared rather than be rushed immediately prior to conducting the RTW:

■ Sick note(s)/certificates appertaining to the current absence, this must include verification that the return-to-work date is accurate.
■ Previous history of sickness and absence (number of days and number of instances) appertaining to the employee for the previous 12 months, and a detailed understanding of the sickness percentage and specific trends (i.e., a trend of repeated absences on a particular day of the week).

- An understanding of the employee's record comparative to his or her colleagues in the depot within the same cadre.
- Any e-mail correspondence history between employee and business, re-read these to refresh your understanding of the history.
- Any disciplinary records associated to sickness and absence, an appreciation of the time lapse since the last "award" and whether the award is "live," or the timeframe has expired and effectively invalid.
- A review of the colleague's personnel file regarding data relevant to the RTW process to provide the interviewer as "rounded" a picture of the colleague as possible.

The RTW interview should be convened between the manager and the colleague in a private and quiet setting. It is not a disciplinary hearing so neither party requires a witness.

Each company will create its own RTW documentation to be completed at the RTW interview and latterly maintained as a formal record, but Figure 1.7 provides a guideline.

Driver Debrief

Chapter 5 is dedicated to driver debrief but an introduction in "People Management" is pertinent as the task provides the pivotal communication point, and which is formal, between management and the driving colleague, and takes place daily at close of the working shift (the duration of which is in the range of 5–15 minutes). Debrief reflects an essential interface that may otherwise not take place given the mobile nature of a driver's role. Warehouse, cleaning, stores, and administrative staff work entirely at the depot and therefore management can interact at will and "in-person" with this captive audience at any time during the day.

One reason some people seek driving roles is a preference to "work alone" and or not to work in a confined space or single place of work, which they may perceive as restrictive and an environment where they may be subject to "micro-management"; but with the advent of driver related technology (PDAs, vehicle telematics, and mobiles) and with the need for businesses to continually improve output, for best results, management teams need to measure driver productivity throughout the day and formally once each day (debrief), and such an environment may be perceived by some as in conflict with their preference to work "independently." Debrief ensures the dual function of bridging the communication gap with drivers whilst providing a structured environment that gathers requisite route and colleague data daily and in a positive environment if the process is conducted well, and which will also provide a platform from which management is able to maintain a participative interest in driver well-being. It is an essential management discipline in any depot employing driving colleagues, and a topic that warrants a dedicated chapter.

Conducting Disciplinaries

Most operational managers will unfortunately conduct multiple disciplinary hearings during their career, it can be a daunting process for some but is a necessary mechanism that supports improvement in colleague attitude and or performance and resolves unacceptable behaviour in the workplace; however, it is heartening to recognise that the majority of employees never participate in a disciplinary process; in a similar vein to absence trends, management's focus is likely to be with a relatively small percentage of the employee base.

In any business with a depot infrastructure, 80%–90% of the employees are likely to work at or from a depot, with the DM and teams effectively having line responsibility for the vast majority of company colleagues. Good businesses will shoulder the responsibility for training depot management teams to ensure that they have relevant knowledge of employment law and the requisite skills required to know how best to conduct the disciplinary process. Local management have a personal responsibility to ensure they are fully conversant with all company procedures (including a detailed understanding of all employee contracts, the Employee Handbook, and any other relevant company literature) so that they are best prepared and able to explain and or dispel the myriad of "urban myths" that inevitably swirl around in the depot environment, partly fuelled by ignorance or a colleague's partial understanding of the detail contained within the contract and handbook. Should a disciplinary process ultimately end up at an Employment Tribunal (ET), they (the local management team) will positively influence the outcome of the tribunal if they have been technically proficient, applied the company terms and conditions to the letter, and are meticulous with detail and note taking throughout each stage of the disciplinary process.

Conducting a formal disciplinary hearing is neither easy nor pleasant, the dry-mouth and nervous instinctive rushing through a hearing is common in the novice, but with good preparation and a structured plan and with practice, the manager's confidence and experience will grow and the process will become less daunting.

The employee has the right (in some instances and depending on length of service) if dismissed, to appeal the final outcome that is delivered by the business and thereafter seek redress via an ET if the employee believes the decision was unfair, the process was not technically properly conducted or if victimisation of some description has taken place. Having to attend and give evidence at an ET is not of itself cause for concern, the process provides independent arbitration for all UK employees and is there to provide protection if businesses act inappropriately. The ET judge is essentially making a judgement as to the reasonableness or otherwise of the process followed by company management and that the subsequent outcome (usually dismissal) was reasonable and appropriate, and to ensure that the process followed by the company was technically sound, lawful, and mirrored the company's policies and procedures exactly. The author has attended several ETs and found the process to be balanced and the outcome fair. However, ET judges do not look favourably on companies or managers that have not adhered exactly to their own stated procedures or present sloppy data or do not have a detailed grasp of the data that is contained in the evidence "pack" they submitted. Be aware that evidence packs formulated by each side is shared in full with the other side ahead of the ET hearing.

In common law, the burden of proof rests with the prosecution to prove guilt, the defendant is deemed innocent until proven guilty, with employment law the verdict is based on "reasonableness" of decision making taking into account the contract and employee handbook, managements' actions in relation to the employment contract, the integrity of documented transactions, the disciplinary steps taken throughout the process, and adherence to company procedures and policies by both the management and the employee.

The author's top-ten tips to follow:

1. Adhere meticulously to company guidelines and the company Handbook including all disciplinary procedures. Usually, these procedures will include set timelines (number of days) to notify of a hearing date(s) and issue of response letter(s) regarding the outcome, adhere meticulously to such clauses to avoid any insinuation that the process which management followed was technically flawed.

2. When conducting a disciplinary hearing, always allow the employee the right of a witness (this will be a fellow employee or union representative, no friend or external associate is normally permitted) and ensure that the convening manager has either a member of HR or management team in attendance to act as their witness and to write meticulous notes of the meeting. The manager's witness should not be of a more senior rank than the convening manager. If the employee declines to have a witness present, ensure they sign and date a statement (or prepared document) to corroborate their decision, to avoid a latter claim that they were denied a witness. Having a witness is not mandatory, but is good practice, and in many companies mandatory, failure to offer the employee a witness is frowned upon at ET.

3. The meeting notes are very likely to be referenced at ET, so it is worthwhile to re-write them immediately post meeting to ensure they are legible and fully accurate, typed is better than handwriting, and it is helpful if they are written in a format that clearly identifies who (manager or colleague) said what. The manager should sign and date and this document which also needs to be read, dated, and signed by the colleague facing discipline. This process verifies that the notes reflect an accurate representation of what was stated by all parties attending the meeting. Before ending a meeting, include a "pause," and request that the person being interviewed together with their witness, leave the room to give you time to collect your thoughts and deliberate on what has been discussed. This period of reflection should be 10–15 minutes minimum. Even if you are sure of the outcome, conduct this "time of reflection," it reflects good practice. The "scribe" must log these times in the meeting notes. Use the time to summarise your thoughts and write a bullet-point summary and outcome that you will deliver when the meeting reconvenes. If upon reflection, more evidence or data is required, do not be reticent in reconvening the disciplinary meeting for a future date but be transparent as to the reasons why, and what further evidence will be collated and reviewed.

4. Be cognisant of what you write in every e-mail, and to who, from the beginning and throughout case, be cognisant from the very beginning until an ET is finalised that employees have the right to request e-mail history. Keep all e-mail language pertinent and professional, avoid expressing personal views and any word or phrase that someone else may perceive as derogatory or inflammatory. If you have a complex or

sensitive point that warrants discussion or clarification, then communicate via a call with your line manager or HR.

5. In the case of a dismissal, the colleague may not be at work therefore all communication will usually be via post, always send via "special delivery" and "signed for" to ensure the business can evidence exactly what was posted and when, this prevents the "I never received" accusation which is not uncommon, and which adds delay to the process and enables unnecessary and unfruitful "deflection" tactics and accusations in later meetings.

6. The disciplinary hearing outcome is linked to the level of planning and preparation time that the convening manager exerts. Do not underestimate the time it may take to collate various documents, e-mails, medical records, review personnel files and verify timelines, dates, and ensure that all relevant witness statements are completed. The better the preparation, the more confident the manager and the more straightforward the outcome. Make a bullet-point plan of exactly what you need to discuss and in what order, and check the list before closing the meeting, failure to do this is likely to result in something pertinent not being raised, even for experienced managers.

7. Share copies of the gathered data that is going to be discussed at the hearing with the employee, this data is not a secret, and ensure the employee has reasonable time (the company disciplinary process will usually stipulate this timeline) to read and digest this data before the hearing. If company timelines are missed, don't press ahead but pause and ensure the process catches up, again avoid the technical flaw accusation.

8. When conducting a hearing do not be phased or concerned if some evidence or if any point is raised that in your view warrants further investigation, it is better to ensure a fair and reasonable outcome than to rush the process. Pause proceedings if warranted and reconvene the hearing and give yourself adequate time to thoroughly investigate and remember once again, to share the findings before recommencing the process.

9. If the case has a technical element (e.g. a vehicle accident or mechanical engine failure due to driver neglect) or health and safety implication (the colleague actions contravened the business H&S procedures), take the time to refer to and involve the right "touch point" in the business to ensure that comprehensive evidence is gathered before commencing the process and this may involve the company health and safety

manager, fleet manager, or another functional support manager, and if pertinent seek opinion (and formal report) from an independent expert body (e.g. Logistics UK Association – formerly the FTA). All involved parties need to formulate individual reports and or statements which are signed and dated, added to the document bundle, and shared with the employee.

10. Verify with HR if a precedent has been previously established in the business with a similar case type and determine if and why this case may guide your thinking, avoid setting a new company precedent and adhere strictly to written company policy, apply logical thinking, and remain calm but focused throughout the process.

Calculating Driver Resource

Figure 1.8 provides a worked example of the calculation required to plan driver resource (driver establishment); this process is aligned to the fleet calculation example discussed in Chapter 2, section "Calculating the Fleet Size" in tandem with Figure 2.1.

	DEPOT "X"		April	May	June	July	Aug	Sept	Oct	Nov	Dec	Jan	Feb	Mar
1														
2		Current	C+1	C+2	C + 3	C + 4	C + 5	C + 6	C + 7	C + 8	C + 9	C + 10	C +11	C + 12
3	Drops / month	20000	21896	19992	21044	21250	19150	21350	21350	24396	21488	21594	19604	22496
4	Working days	21	23	21	22	23	21	22	22	23	19	22	20	23
5	Ave depot routes per weekday	38	38	38	38	37	37	39	39	41	44	39	39	39
6	Driver resource requirement													
7	Base driver establishment	38	38	38	38	37	37	39	39	39	39	39	39	39
8	Holiday @ 8%	4	4	5	5	5	5	4	4	0	0	4	4	4
9	Absence @ 3%	1	1	1	1	1	1	1	1	1	1	1	1	1
10	Sub total	43	43	43	43	42	42	44	44	40	40	44	44	44
11	Leavers (25%)	1	1	1	1	1	1	1	1	1	0	1	1	1
12	Starters (in training)	1	1	1	1	1	2	1	1	1	0	1	1	1
13	Adjusted gross total	44	44	44	44	44	44	45	45	45	45	45	45	45
14	Available net trained drivers	38	38	38	38	38	37	39	39	42	44	39	39	39
15	Balancing figure	0	0	-1	-1	0	0	0	0	+1	0	0	0	0
16	Potential agency hire	0	0	0	0	0	1	0	0	2	2	0	0	0
17	Estimated OT %	8%	8%	10%	10%	10%	10%	8%	8%	15%	15%	5%	7%	8%

Figure 1.8   Example of driver resource forward planner.

The drops per month (row 3) is key data as all other metrics cascade from this number. Ensuring that the forward data is credible and accurate is essential. Operations must collate the future growth predictions in as much detail as is feasible from either or both the Sales and Financial departments, and this data must also incorporate known customer losses and known contract wins that start at some point during the plan, this will ensure that the number in row 3 is a net number, scientifically calculated, and formally verified by the Finance department. Conduct sensitivity analysis and examine historical data regarding estimating predictable peak trading months. If the drop volume data is inaccurate or as accurate as Finance/Sales can guarantee it, so will the resource planner be. Consider including a supplementary row (beneath row 3) to provide for a "contingency" volume row if the business has a low level of certainty regarding volume and mirror this contingency row with additional drivers (below row 16) to compensate.

The drop volume and average number of routes per day is identical to that used in the fleet calculation example. Row 5 (average routes per day) reflects the number of average planned routes, and therefore, vehicles that are required to operate from the depot each weekday. The requisite number is generated by the route planners (scheduler). In the example, weekend working is negligible and is assumed to be covered by overtime working (row 17) not fulltime employees. In practice depot management will need to produce more granular versions of this template, by day, week, and month. Figure 1.9 illustrates what row 5 from Figure 1.8 might look like in a weekly format. The average number of 38 in Figure 1.8 is more nuanced in Figure 1.9 row 3. This granularity will be required for each row incorporated in Figure 1.8 with additional rows for actual and variance (plan vs. actual).

The weekly plan is further broken down to individual day as illustrated in Figure 1.10. This will enable management, schedulers, and drivers to understand planned activity to the driver level and performance against plan at the end of the day. Each operational team will determine the data set required to formulate the KPIs that will best measure service quality and productivity. In the example, the four key categories are:

Service	Missed drops and % achievement of actual over plan.
Worked hours	Planned vs. paid hours.
Miles driven	Planned route miles vs. actual driven.
Key ratios	Drops per hour and miles per drop.

1	DEPOT "X"	Week 1 – April						Week 2 – April					
2		Mon	Tue	Wed	Thurs	Fri	Sat	Mon	Tue	Wed	Thurs	Fri	Sat
3	Routes per day	39	38	37	38	38	4	39	38	37	37	39	3
4	Actual routes per day	39	38	38	38	38	5	39	38	37	37	40	3
5	Variance to plan	0	0	1	0	0	1	0	0	0	0	1	0

Figure 1.9   Planned vs. actual routes – weeks one and two – April.

DEPOT "X"	Week 1 - Monday routes									Ratios	
	Drops plan	Drops Act	Missed	% Complete	Hours plan	Hours act	Variance	Miles plan	Miles act	Drops per hr	Miles per drop
Route 1 Driver A	24	23	1	96%	9	9	0	130	136	2.5	5.9
Route 2 Driver B	26	24	2	92%	9	8.75	(0.25)	138	148	2.7	6.1
Route 39 Driver BK	22	22	0	100%	9.25	9.5	0.25	152	154	2.3	7

Figure 1.10   Example of daily route data.

These KPIs will enable comparative analysis between drivers and depot performance and measure the scheduler's (planner) skill to route plan. For further reference to KPIs, including a suite of guideline KPIs, refer to Chapter 8, "KPIs, the Balance Scorecard, and Basic Financial Models."

Figure 1.8 illustrates the benefit of having a structured forward holiday plan. In the example, known peak trading (November and December) requires additional driver resources to operate additional peak routes, and this is largely covered through implementing a red-ring (zero holiday) policy which generates an additional net two to three drivers each month during this period, and the surplus holiday days generated by the red-ring policy are utilised in turn to bolster the summer peak driver demand during the school holiday season. This holiday plan suppresses the requirement for additional OT and or agency drivers and ensures that experienced drivers are used to carry the operation through peak trading. The residue shortfall (row15 – Figure 1.8) will be covered firstly with increased overtime combined with a tweaking of routes (schedulers should be able to increase drops-per-route productivity as volume density improves) to lengthen the working day slightly, with any unforeseen additional driver requirements will be supplemented with agency.

In order to fulfil an average of 38 routes (first half of the year – H1) and 39 routes in H2 to compensate for budgeted volume growth, an establishment of 44 drivers moving to 45 is required, the rationale is as follows:

- An average of four drivers need to be taking holiday each month (row 8). If holidays are not managed effectively and the min–max rule not applied, the number of drivers taking leave each month may fluctuate significantly and this would render overall resource planning less predictable and likely to increase overtime or agency requirements and associated costs to compensate if holiday "spiking" occurs.
- The depot is budgeting c3% absence (row 9) equating to an average of one driver each period. With diligent absent management controls, the 3% is deemed achievable and baked into the plan; however, if the absence trend is out of kilter and the absence figure rises, the base establishment figure will need to rise in equal number or add further agency into the mix to compensate and thereby increase costs.
- It is important to understand the attrition trend on a per depot basis when resource planning, depot X in the example has an attrition rate of c25% (11/44) which equates on average to one driver per month (row 11) except December (in the example, the business has experienced zero leavers as colleagues tend to avoid change, and focus on maximising their earnings pre-Christmas), that will leave the business.
- The budget (forward) plan must incorporate new starters to maintain equilibrium, one new starter will join each month (row 12); however, in this plan, the new starter is not considered fully productive and therefore able to drive a route unaided and achieve optimum productivity (average drops per route achieved) for one full month.
- In row 12, an additional driver (2) is recruited in August to increase base establishment in preparation for the uplift in volume for H2.
- November and December have increased peak trading volume, and in the example, business management counter this predictable peak with a zero-holiday policy as described in detail above.
- Rows 16 and 17 represent the operational tactic to provide a short-term boost to compensate for any unexpected event, for example an increased trend regarding holiday, absence, attrition. The application of OT is preferred to agency staff as the latter are less conversant with the job, less emotionally invested in the business and its customers, and reflect a higher cost per hour (due to the supplier's profit element) to the company than a fulltime employee. Some businesses may not

be able to deploy agency staff due to security certification or customer vetting standards, or because the operation or fleet are too specialised. The caveat however, with applying OT as the primary lever to bolster the establishment level, is that the application is allowed to become normalised and not just a short-term measure, there are various reasons why this happens but if allowed to normalise colleagues become dependent personally on higher earnings and management may encounter resistance if and when management wish to reduce OT levels in order, for example to become more cost effective, it is important therefore to maintain establishment numbers and the starting point to achieving this key goal is to have a coherent and detailed resource plan.

Notes

1. Office of National Statistics UK. Labour.market@ons.gov.uk. 3 March 2021. Debra Leaker and Karen Kumar.
2. Bradford factor. (1) Lindsay, Kali (5 October 2017). "What is the Bradford Factor, and can you be sacked for being sick too much?" Chronicle Live. (2) HR News (5 May 2016). Adrian Lewis. "What HR needs to know about the Bradford Factor."

Chapter 2

Fleet Management

Introduction

Without fleet (commercial vehicles) a logistics organisation cannot exit, and fleet is usually the second highest operating cost (it may be the highest in specialist logistics businesses) in any route-based logistics company. Commercial vehicles (HGV or LCV) have a finite economic life budgeted for by applying depreciation costs, the lifespan of a commercial vehicle can range from four years (small high-mileage LCV) to ten years depending on the model type and average annual mileage, with some businesses conducting a mid-life refurbishment to extend the working life of the vehicle. Businesses have to invest capital (or enter into contract lease deals) annually to introduce a proportion of new fleet to maintain an efficient and reliable road-worthy operation with a blend of older and new vehicles.

SMEs aside, many modern national service providers operate fleet sizes that range from one hundred to the tens of thousands, and to maintain the fleet (total number of vehicles) at optimum cost requires meticulous management by expert fleet managers with appropriate sector credentials. Fleet management involves the orchestration of multiple "moving parts" with the fleet leadership team having to oversee internal depot management teams, driving colleagues, external fleet manufacturers, fleet management support companies (suppliers) responsible for insurance, breakdown, recovery, vehicle hire, and workshops whether in-house or third party. Additionally, fuel needs purchasing (a joint task in tandem with the Finance department) with a sizeable proportion of litres purchased annually "hedged" in advance to control cost. This team will oversee fleet storage (placement and care of

DOI: 10.4324/9781003323822-2

spare vehicles), and on-the-road vehicle monitoring via telematics, to help prevent misuse and to provide early warning of possible engine deterioration or identify poor driving standards.

Fleet management is a specialist management discipline which incorporates the head of the department to be responsible for licencing (the "O" or operator's licence) of vehicles (in excess of 3.5 tonnes) on behalf of the company. There may be legal licence requirements and driver qualifications depending on the vehicle specification and load carried, for example chemicals or hazardous materials. From a health and safety (H&S) perspective, the most severe employee accidents are likely to be fleet related (RTA – road traffic accident) and it is the arm of the business where an employee (driver) may become involved with a third party (a member of the public or customer) or damage customer property. In the event of an RTA resulting in a fatality, the impact to the business and management team will be intrusive, challenging, may involve interaction with Police, the Health and Safety Executive, insurance companies, loss adjusters and which may endure for several months.

A proportion of all complaints from either the public and or customers are likely to emanate from poor driving standards, vehicle incidents, illegal parking, or damage to a member of the public's vehicle (whether genuine or not). The number of incidents of false claims is increasing annually and fleet management teams need robust procedures to deal with effectively with this problem, whilst administering the stream of parking tickets that occur weekly, especially in urban street parking (specifically London boroughs with Bus Lane CCTV, Red-routes, Double Yellow-lines, and a host of street parking restrictions) with some boroughs particularly adept at targeting the "captive" market of commercial fleets as they go about their business.

To cap this array of tasks, businesses operating in London are likely to require FORS certification, an onerous responsibility and time-consuming task for fleet management teams that will include internal and external (governing body) audits.

Calculating the Fleet Size

This is a fundamental process requiring collaboration between fleet, operations, and scheduling management teams and the exercise requires regular review (at least quarterly) to ensure minimum waste and to ensure accuracy of forward planning and will take the following data into consideration, known new business volume, organic growth, and customer contraction (lost drops/services). The calculation needs building "bottom-upwards" on a depot-by-depot basis to be most accurate as volume (number of customer drop) will be nuanced geographically.

At its most basic level, the calculation is illustrated in Figure 2.1. This simple example illustrates a single depot (Depot X). In Figure 2.1, the entire depot drop-volume is delivered via a single vehicle model type, but if there were multiple vehicle models (i.e., the product or equipment being carried requires a different vehicle specification, for example due to weight capacity) then the drop-volume would need splitting accurately by model type with the number of jobs per vehicle also split by type.

A point of contention (between depot and fleet management) may be the allocation of the spare vehicle(s); in Figure 2.1, one spare vehicle is required, but it may be necessary to incorporate a spare per model derivative, and this decision may be influenced by the ease of attaining a direct hire replacement. Some vehicle types cannot be readily replicated via hire businesses and therefore the "spare" (contingency) number required will increase.

The calculation to establish fleet is different from determining the driver establishment (see Chapter 1, "People Management," Figures 1.8–1.10).

To aid orientation with Figure 2.1:

■ The average drops per working day (row 6) reflect total drops (row 3) less drops completed at weekends, supplementary work (work requiring no additional base fleet) divided by the number of weekday days in the period. Bank holidays are excluded if not worked.
■ The average number of drops per route (row 7) completed per day is a critical number. It will vary by depot due to geographical variations and density of work (i.e., a depot servicing London will have a significantly higher average drop per route per day than a rural depot located in Aberdeen or Norfolk). This number must be accurate, and when forecasting, it is important to incorporate planned improvement via productivity initiatives (for simplicity, the example has no improvement trend) being planned in the future, and additionally consider the impact of peak-period volume. In Figure 2.1, both November and December have higher drops per day per route because the density (the average miles between each drop locations) improves (reduces) as the number of drops increase.
■ Row 11 (base fleet) reflects the actual number of vehicles Depot X is estimated to require including a percentage to cover VOR and spare.

	DEPOT "X"		April	May	June	July	Aug	Sept	Oct	Nov	Dec	Jan	Feb	Mar
1		Current	C+1	C+2	C+3	C+4	C+5	C+6	C+7	C+8	C+9	C+10	C+11	C+12
2		20000	21896	19992	21044	21250	19150	21350	21350	24396	21488	21594	19604	22496
3	Drops / month	20000	21896	19992	21044	21250	19150	21350	21350	24396	21488	21594	19604	22496
4	Working days	21	23	21	22	23	21	22	22	23	19	22	20	23
5	Drops / month on weekend	700	766	700	737	744	670	747	747	854	752	756	686	787
6	Ave drops per day weekdays	919	919	919	923	892	880	936	936	1024	1091	947	946	944
7	Ave drops per route	24	24	24	24	24	24	24	24	25	25	24	24	24
8	Ave depot routes per weekday	38	38	38	38	37	37	39	39	41	44	39	39	39
9	Variation in Fleet from current	0	0	0	0	(1)	(2)	1	1	3	5	1	1	1
10	**Fleet Plan Depot X (current base position, and forward annual plan)**													
11	Base Fleet	41	41	41	41	41	41	41	41	41	41	41	41	41
12	VOR @ 4%	4%												
13	Est. no. of VOR	2	2	2	2	2	2	2	2	2	2	2	2	2
14	Spare	1	1	1	1	1	1	1	1	1	1	1	1	1
15	Available Fleet	38	38	38	38	38	38	38	38	38	38	38	38	38
16	Est. surplus or shortfall	0	0	0	0	1	2	(1)	(1)	(3)	(5)	(1)	(1)	(1)
17	Est. Hire							1	1	3	5	1	1	1
18	Est. surplus					1	2							
19	Exit run-rate base Fleet													42

Figure 2.1   Example of current and future fleet requirements at Depot "X."

■ Every fleet has vehicles which are unavailable daily (VOR – vehicles off road). These may be planned VOR:
  - Annual or miles-derived service
  - Inspection (for HGV vehicles)
  - Modification (the vehicle body may require renewing or an upgrade in design to improve carrying capacity, for example)
  - At garage under repair (mechanical or bodywork) from a previous day's accident, incident, or breakdown

Or unplanned:

  - Breakdown or accident on the day
  - Unable to start and leave depot
  - Theft or damage overnight (discovered before planned departure)
  - Vehicle defect arising on the day (i.e., shutter doors cease to work effectively)

fleet VOR reporting will reflect both planned and unplanned.

What does "good" VOR look like? Well-run fleet operations working harmoniously with local depot management teams should be able to achieve 96% or better "up-time" with circa 4% down-time (VOR). If a fleet is operating at a low 90% performance or less, for any period of time other than a few working days, there is a fundamental problem that requires addressing. The root cause may reflect poor vehicle asset, supplier, workshop, or daily operating control by fleet and or operational management teams. A sub-95% up-time performance needs addressing quickly to prevent customer service failures and escalating operating costs rise due to increased vehicle hires to compensate, and where hires do not provide a suitable alternative and the number of available vehicles falls below the minimum requirement, driver OT will increase to enable extended route times in order to conduct more services to compensate for reduced overall fleet. Note: If up-time is poor but zero hires are required this implies the base fleet number is too high and incorporating significant capacity (slack).

In the context of Figure 2.1, row 12 incorporates a provision for VOR (with the 4% rounded up not down).

Row 14 incorporates one spare vehicle to provide a cushion to cover those unplanned events outlined above. As a "rule of thumb," 2% (one per 50 vehicles) is recommended as a depot operational spare. If the business determines a higher number of spare vehicles is necessary, it is advised that part of this spare fleet is held centrally and controlled directly by the fleet management team (retained physically in geographically strategic non-depot locations, or if stored at a depot, vehicle keys will be controlled by fleet) to prevent depot teams operating all "spares" housed at the depot without due constraint and management controls.

Row 11 represents the base number of vehicles (41) required to fulfil the daily requirement of 38 including three estimated to cover both VOR and spare representing 8%.

In Figure 2.1, there is overall growth of 3% of drop volume incrementally quarter-by-quarter with a high Christmas peak (November and December). This short-term peak is best (economically) served via short-term hires if the business can effectively carry out services using hire vehicles; in the example, underlying growth culminates in the exit (year-end at March) base fleet run rate being 42 (row 19), an increase of one (row 11) and assuming senior management authorised a vehicle purchase, the plan suggests that it would be best introduced from P6 (September) to help benefit the Christmas volume peak, whilst simultaneously reducing the hire requirement. Note: Where specialised fleet is used rendering hires unusable, the hire-for-Christmas solution is impractical and the minimum base fleet number will need to increase to cover the known peak volume, an effective ploy used previously is to retain otherwise end-of-life fleet in a road-worthy condition, mothball under the auspices of fleet management, and use them solely for the purpose of covering this peak period, incorporating a mechanical "once-over" before issuing to depots.

In Figure 2.1, there is a surplus of fleet for two months (July and August) which illustrates that fleet planning is not exact, the aim is to get the fleet number as close to optimal as is feasible each month with consideration regarding exiting fleet (end of life. Which months do leases and or depreciation expire), new purchases (when best introduced, and working backwards, when to order), hires, spares, and VOR trends. In the example, the surplus is used as a regional spare, or if an ongoing annual replacement programme is in progress, then a couple of vehicles at "end of life" might be released a little early before the planned new vehicle arrives to keep the depot compliment deliberately lean.

Organisational Design

Given the importance of fleet management regarding a business's capacity to be able to deliver on its contractual service commitments, and the need to operate legally in compliance with all government laws, the structure of the fleet team is important to consider and will be linked to the size and complexity of the fleet.

In any fleet with HGVs, or with significant LCV fleets, the senior fleet manager needs to be CPC qualified (Certificate of Professional Competence), and he or she should also be the official O-licence (Operating Licence) holder for the company, this responsibility should not be deferred.

Logistics businesses have varying sizes of fleet, some with several thousand vehicles, and in these cases, the fleet management structure and associated stakeholders are complex. In smaller businesses with a fleet size of sub-500, the positions of fleet manager and fleet design/procurement manager illustrated in Figure 2.2 may be combined; however, if the fleet is of specialist design and or requiring bespoke build modifications, the latter role may prove invaluable.

The fleet function is essentially an integral part of Operations and usually reports directly to the COO or the Operations Director; however, a "dotted line" to the CFO to support procurement, fuel purchase, and "hedging" and

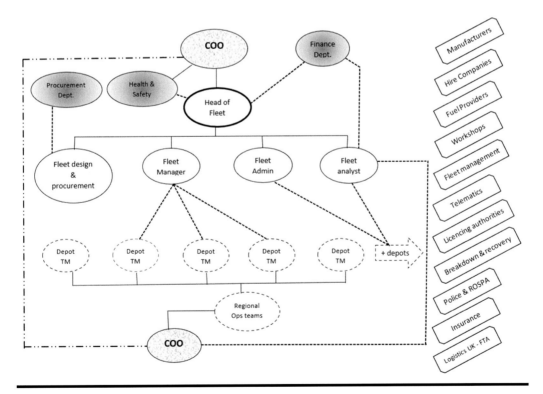

Figure 2.2   Fleet department org. structure.

to be involved with new vehicle purchase and end-of-life disposal is highly recommended.

To function effectively, the fleet team requires significant support and collaboration from other key internal stakeholders including:

■ *Finance*

Working collaboratively with Head of Fleet (HoF) and fleet analyst the Finance department provides periodic (monthly) financial accounts to a granularity including as a minimum the elements below, and reporting actual vs. budget and including updated year-end forecasts. Depreciation and lease costs aside, maintaining the fleet reflects a large ongoing business cost, and these costs rise annually, but in order to have the wherewithal to effectively control and reduce this complex cost base, the HoF must have robust, accurate, and current data of suitable granularity, and whilst it may take time and money to produce, the savings and service benefits will significantly outweigh the cost to produce the requisite data.

– Fuel usage in volume (litres consumed) and monetary terms for period and year to date (YTD) with an average overall cost per mile on a model-by-model basis, ideally split by depot, region, and nationally.

– Accident damage costs by depot and in total and applying a ratio basis per depot miles driven in the period and number of vehicles. Ideally, this data should have a granularity to individual vehicle registration in order to track driver performance. Pareto (the 80/20 rule) suggests a small number of driving colleagues will cause a high percentage of damage and repair costs, but depot management need the data to take remedial action.

– Running costs (all costs) by model type by month and in total, with a ratio providing an average pence-per-mile (ppm) per model type.

– Repairs and Maintenance (R&M) costs (excluding damage) by vehicle and by depot (as a monetary number and as a ratio); additionally, R&M costs are useful split by workshop/garage (whether in-house or third party). The more granular the detail, the easier it is to conduct comparative trends by supplier by key types of work (e.g. gearbox, clutches) and compare key cost elements such as the labour rate charged per hour, which can vary significantly by geography and by individual garage.

If the fleet size exceeds one thousand vehicles, the HoF may require the allocation of a semi-dedicated finance partner to collaborate with the analyst to aid compilation of a period fleet financial pack and to attend the period fleet financial review meeting with COO and CFO.

■ *Health and Safety (H&S)*

Depending on the size and complexity of the business the H&S Department may encompass additional responsibility for: environment, audit, safety related training, compliance and or quality. The Head of H&S is shown in Figure 2.2 as reporting directly to the COO. Companies may have differing structures, the author has known this role to report to the CEO, CFO, and CTO to provide "independence" from Operations and to "police" operational activity; however, the author has had H&S reporting to the COO because 80% to 90% of employees usually work across operational departments and most incidents/accidents befall a colleague working in Operations. If the COO/Operations Director assumes full accountability for H&S (and all associated legal responsibilities) and is seen to be doing so by directly promoting and driving H&S initiatives across all aspects of the operation, the author would argue that best H&S metrics (RIDDOR, LTIFR, near-miss reporting) are achieved with the direct involvement of the COO working collaboratively with the company H&S manager.

■ *Procurement*

It is not good practice for any department to procuring goods, consumables, or products directly without the support and guidance of the procurement team which provides governance and independence to the procurement process. The HoP (Head of Procurement) should report directly to the CFO. There are a myriad of suppliers competing to sell their services and products to fleet teams, and even post the advent of the Bribery Act, the mandatory inclusion of procurement for all fleet procurement projects is prudent.

The Head of Fleet

This is a critical role to fill and should be filled with the highest calibre individual the company can secure relative to the size and complexity of fleet. Branson stated that businesses should "train people well enough so they can leave but treat them well enough, so they don't want to." High calibre senior fleet leaders are not at all easy to find or to recruit, and too many are ex-workshop engineers that have migrated to management over time without losing their yearning for the "oily-rag." Securing a fully rounded professional manager with excellent negotiating and people-leadership qualities coupled with expertise in all things mechanical is like finding "chickens' teeth." Excluding the senior Operations leader (Operations Director or COO), arguably the Head of Fleet is the key role to secure and retain but challenging to find for any business with high fleet numbers; get it wrong and the fleet will operate at suboptimal cost, may unknowingly breach legal requirements on occasion, and customer service is likely to be sub-standard.

The Two Sides of Fleet Organisational Design

The fleet team have two broad stakeholder groups to collaborate with and manage and these are internal (other company colleagues and departments) and external stakeholders.

Internal Stakeholders

The primary internal relationship is with Operations line management and by association all driving colleagues with the objective to ensure that:

1. The fleet (number of vehicles) is maintained at optimal levels (refer Figure 2.1) and to avoid unnecessary "creep" of excess new vehicles and or surplus hire.
2. The fleet is maintained in compliance with all legal and statutory standards and is operated safely (both driven safely by colleagues and vehicles are maintained to meet the highest safety standards).
3. The VOR target of 96% up-time and secondary "72-hour workshop" target (see Chapter 8, KPIs section, Figure 8.2) is maintained or bettered.
4. That incremental and continuous improvement is achieved at the depot and nationally, regarding the following trends:
   a. Number and type of accidents/incidents,
   b. Servicing and inspections completed to scheduled programmes,
   c. Unit costs per vehicle/depot regarding running, damage, and parts costs are all maintained to budget.

Best practice will ensure that every depot manager responsible for commercial fleet is a current holder of a CPC (this may take time to implement but is highly recommended) and in large depots (50 plus vehicles) a member of the management team deemed partly or fully responsible for local "Fleet Management" and this person may be appointed as the designated CPC "holder," but this should not negate the requirement for the depot manager to be duly trained. Management CPC courses are held at least twice each year and for best results block-book a full week's training and preparation immediately prior to the exam so the copious data intake remains fresh and relevant.

The depot management team need to own accountability for upholding legislative and good practice fleet protocol. A small central fleet team can provide business procedures, create a robust contractual foundation with external third parties (for example, local workshop garages including operating hours, pricing, labour rates, annual audits, etc.) and provide guidance to the local team but depot management must do the day-to-day "heavy-lifting" of promoting and enforcing company fleet protocol. The central fleet team will collate daily fleet KPI data and produce (independent of local depots) company fleet statistics, trends, and performance. Where individual depots or managers are underperforming against plan or found not to be adhering to company protocol the fleet team must escalate, and in tandem with senior Operations line management, address the root cause.

The fundamental top ten "must-do" fleet tasks, in association with local management include the following elements, note that driver debrief is the cornerstone of driver communication and it is assumed mandatory and not included in this list, but refer Chapter 5 which is dedicated to driver debrief:

1. Ensure that every *vehicle is serviced and inspected* (HGV) strictly in line with the agreed service schedule between central fleet team, depot, and local workshop.
2. Ensure that every driver conducts a formal *daily vehicle check* and that the driver confirms this process, which is validated during driver debrief.
3. Ensure that drivers are specifically asked if there are any vehicle *defects to report* at the end of every working shift, and formally record a "zero defects" declaration if no defects are present. A reported defect needs to be verified within 24 hours and addressed quickly via an evidenced-based audit trail of what, when, and by whom the defect was rectified.
4. Every vehicle *accident* is to be recorded and reported in accordance with company procedure and must be fully and formally investigated

by local management within a target of 24 hours post accident (excluding weekends) and if appropriate (the damage or accident type is severe), the local depot team may require support from the central fleet team.

5. Ensure that a *physical vehicle inspection is conducted weekly* with both driver and a member of management present for every commercial vehicle located at depot. For best results, a photograph is taken of the four sides of the vehicle and checked against the previous week's photographs (maintain a record per vehicle registration per driver) to verify that no unreported damage/accident has taken place. This process can be cross-referenced with driver defect reports. If a vehicle has been re-issued to another driver mid-week, it is in the new driver's interest to report any defect and or damage on the first day of receiving the vehicle, and before it is driven on the road, in order to absolve him or her of any subsequent blame. Where a vehicle is exchanged at depot, management should be present at hand-over. Unreported accidents and vehicle defects do warrant a formal review and may result in disciplinary action as unreported issues may, in a worst-case scenario, prove to be a root cause latterly in an incident which may potentially have grave consequences (if a serious RTA) for the second driver of the vehicle and or a third party, and by association depot management.

6. Ensure that *tachographs (HGV) and driver hours* are correctly applied, completed accurately and fully recorded and verified, with infringements recorded and discussed formally with offending drivers.

7. Ensure that driver *fuel records* (whether via depot bunker or fuel card) are maintained and accurately recorded.

8. That *driver licence checks* (the actual licence must be checked by management not a copy) are completed at least annually and ideally six-monthly where drivers have a known licence points-record.

9. That *driver CPC courses* are scheduled, attended, and recorded to ensure compliance with the law. The business needs to take accountability for this process regardless of the requirement for drivers to comply themselves; local management diligence will ensure company compliance and help management avoid absence "spiking" as a direct result of driver CPC course "indiscipline."

10. That *telematics data* is reviewed daily by management with constructive feedback (both positive and negative) given to every driver at driver debrief (see the *Telematics* section below).

External Stakeholders

Figure 2.2 illustrates the key external suppliers and stakeholders that fleets deal with on a day-to-day basis; the variety and complexity of stakeholders reinforces the need for businesses to recruit an experienced leader with commercial fleet experience and rounded skill set.

FTA (Logistics UK)

Membership to this organisation is a "must-do" for all logistics organisations and senior fleet management (irrespective of size) to ensure that the fleet team are kept up to date with current and future changes to commercial fleet legislation. This organisation is widely known, respected, and provides specialist support to businesses irrespective of size. The FTA are particularly helpful in providing (at a cost) expert independent assessments/investigations, including a formal judgement, post a serious accident or vehicle mechanical incident in diagnosing the root cause and recommending remedial works post complex mechanical failures and repairs.

Breakdown and Recovery

There are limited businesses capable of providing reliable and consistent roadside breakdown and recovery service on a nationwide basis and therefore prices tend to be high, but procurement leverage improves the larger the fleet. During contract negotiation with a recovery supplier, the procuring party will benefit from taking time to ensure that the SLAs (service level agreements) are robust in order to secure the best possible service provision post contract signing, tips include the following:

- Providers tend to want to agree an "average" time of arrival or apply a percentage of attendances within a given time (i.e., 80% or 90% within 60 minutes of the recorded call). Ensure the contract incorporates a "back-stop" time to prevent the "tail" (final 5% of attendances) stretching to several hours' duration. Apply something like "90% within 60 minutes and 100% within 120 minutes" and include penalties for not achieving targets.
- Understand the number of recovery drivers and vehicles that the provider employees in each geographical region to sense-check the

"promised" time of arrival. Few providers are genuinely 100% national in their geographical service footprint and are likely therefore to use a variety of subcontractors in remote areas (and in these cases, all suppliers are likely to use the same small, often independent third party, and this is likely to impact service times); understand the communication process between primary and secondary provider, the hours of work of the secondary provider and whether the SLAs agreed with the primary provider are genuinely "back-to-back" with the secondary provider or whether less robust SLAs apply. The most remote third-party areas include Scottish "Highlands and Islands," Central and North Wales, Cornwall, possibly Norfolk, Anglesey, Isle of Wight, and Isle of Man.

■ Understand whether the supplier operates a triage service when receiving the initial call request (it is useful if these calls are recorded for review in the event of a "dispute") from the driver, triage is helpful to determine the root cause and to determine whether a "road-side" (smaller vehicle and technician) is mostly like to resolve the breakdown, or whether a recovery vehicle is needed to "lift and shift" (transport) the vehicle directly to a garage. Some logistics businesses have specialist vehicles and or cargo that renders the "road-side" solution inappropriate. In the event that a "lift and shift" solution is required, the business and provider must ensure that the latter retains a "current" list of fleet registrations, including the GVW (gross vehicle weight) to ensure that the assigned recovery vehicle is of requisite specification and capable of carrying the vehicle being recovered, otherwise a second vehicle will need to be despatched and many hours wasted.

■ Negotiate a target "time-to-fix" (ETF) which means attend and fix, so the time to get the breakdown vehicle actually moving once again, avoid agreeing only a target time to arrive (ETA). Less scrupulous providers, and occasionally more reputable suppliers during peak time may send a roadside vehicle to satisfy the ETA target, only to then facilitate a lift and shift. This scenario may also take place where no triage process takes place, or the call handler is inexperienced.

■ For businesses with specialist fleet or 1,000 plus vehicles negotiate the inclusion of a dedicated call-handling team which receive training from the procuring business in order to understand the nuances of the fleet, it helps if this dedicated team visit a depots as part of their training and have a guided tour of the vehicle models where they are specialist, the more time is taken to educate this team the less errors will occur out of hours when, between driver and handler the business needs them to make "the right call" regarding the most appropriate solution.

Telematics

There are a myriad of suppliers selling telematics solutions and many "urban myths" regarding the benefit and potential bottom-line savings to businesses in deploying telematics. The author has deployed telematics solutions across 15,000 plus vehicles (of various gross weights and model specifications) spanning four businesses in the UK and across Europe, the learning from this is outlined below.

Is Telematics Worth Implementing?

From a profitability perspective, the answer to this question is that it depends entirely on what price the business pays the supplier for installation, rental (or purchase), and for ongoing "licencing" and data report production including any subsequent refinements to. Before starting any contract discussion with a prospective supplier, the business must calculate accurately for its own fleet (by model type) what it spends on fuel on a per month basis per vehicle. This exercise provides an important baseline.

Telematics rental prices can vary wildly between suppliers and the author has worked in businesses which had previously negotiated the contract, at rental prices that were higher than the weekly saving delivered post implementation. This is simply wasting money.

Suppliers "promise" and promote a wide range of percentage savings from introducing telematics so proceed with caution. There are two phases with telematics, an immediate gain post introduction, and then incremental opportunity that requires hard work and diligence to deliver. It is important that the contract incorporates a minimum saving guarantee and thereafter a share (between supplier and procurer) of incremental savings achieved from the base position to reflect a genuine win-win solution for both parties, and to ensure that the telematics provider has "skin in the game" and is prepared to jointly work hard to deliver benefit. Ensure before signing any contract that operational managers appreciate how telematics work, and they as managers will be expected to do in order to achieve optimum results, it is *not* a plug and play solution. Post implementation, suppliers can be quick to challenge any failure to achieve the "promised" percentage improvement and blame the business operations teams for failing to own and deliver, and accusations are likely to be, but not limited to: drivers tampering with equipment, the initial "baseline" data was inaccurate, local depot management not fully engaged in daily briefings, local management not conducting daily feedback sessions with requisite enthusiasm … and so on.

It is fundamental to understand that any telematics offering is not a "plug-and-play" solution. The potential percentage savings outlined below are achievable, but it requires complete buy-in from business management (especially depot teams) and is time absorbing, which is often not fully appreciated by businesses where managers have not used telematics previously, or who have been enticed with the salesperson promise of high-percentage savings. Establishing an accurate "before introduction" baseline position is essential. Without commitment, hard work, and focus from management teams during implementation and on an ongoing basis, savings to baseline may be negligible, and the actual cost in management time is not always considered when calculating the business case. Always conduct a pilot to prove principle at a single depot (large urban depot recommended) where the depot management team are experienced, of high calibre, and importantly want to be at the vanguard and use the learning from the pilot as the template for future rollout once it has been perfected and the wrinkles fully ironed out. The supplier will need to be fully engaged through this process regarding installation, calibration (and re-calibration) of the "black box," training (and re-training) of management, and developing and finessing reports and statistics that are pertinent to the business.

Once the "black box" is installed each vehicle, model type will need to be calibrated by the provider to achieve a standard setting for each model. *It is essential that post calibration the telematics solution is switched on "silently" (so that the driver is unaware, with the in-cab buzzer/dashboard inactive, and driver feedback-back sessions are not conducted) continue "silent running" for a period of four to six weeks to establish an accurate baseline from which future improvement, or otherwise, can be measured.* When "switching on a depot" and switching off "silent running" do this as a whole depot and not piecemeal driver by driver as this method will skew the baseline position. It is recommended the switch-on date coincides with day-one of a new financial period to ensure a "clean" set of results and one each month can be compared to another.

The consistent findings across a decade (2010–2020) of telematics deployment is that:

1. Broadly speaking, the percentage of fuel savings improve as the gross vehicle weight increases. LCVs sub-1,000 kgs have a modest saving expectation of c3%–5%; however, other associated benefits (see point 3 below) may render installation worthwhile across the long term if the telematics rental price per unit is modest.
2. Fuel savings in larger vans and HGV vehicles in fleets where telematics have not previously been installed may range from 8% to 12%, with some businesses achieving as high as 15%–16% if the fleet has been ineffectively managed, and where local management buy-in to the process is enthusiastic and persistent.
3. Associated benefits derived from introduction include the following. The improvement is tangible but less straightforward to quantify precisely as the following elements may be contributable by other factors and not solely via telematics:
    i.   A significant reduction in driver incidences of speeding (c10%–15% range) which directly assists in reducing fuel consumption and road accidents.
    ii. Wear and tear of tyres is improved and reduced over time.
    iii. With accident trends improving, the numbers and cost of accident replacement and repaired parts will reduce. Note, accident reduction is largely achieved in RTAs, not reversing or other slow speed "yard-type" manoeuvres.
    iv. The carbon footprint of the business (in road-transport operations fuel consumption is often the highest single contributary factor to producing carbon) will be reduced.
    v.   Management benefit from an enriched data set from telematics and technical linkage to scheduling software that together help provide stronger KPI data. Note, some providers may try to sell a combined telematics and scheduling package, but it is important when considering scheduling software to conduct a specific, standalone tender exercise to procure the scheduling software package that is most appropriate to the operation (see Chapter 3).
    vi. If managed robustly telematics will enhance health and safety of drivers and indirectly other road users. This H&S linkage, in tandem with improved emissions output, provide the rationale that management can use for promoting telematics implementation in situations where unions and or work colleagues may be sceptical of a new process that may be perceived as being intrusive given the in-cab interaction and intensified data feedback regime.

What Is Telematics?

It is a manufactured telemetry unit (sometimes called a "black box") that is fitted to a vehicle and linked with the CANbus (in more modern vehicles). The technology has been on the market for decades via multiple suppliers, but the reporting and management software packages are much improved since 2010, but the data report packs vary hugely supplier by supplier. The technology records vehicle movement in real time and provides alerts of each incidence of harsh braking, harsh cornering, and harsh acceleration. A dashboard is fitted in-cab to give driver feedback with a RAG light system and optional in-cab "buzzer" (recommended) that sounds at each "harsh" event. Note, during the weekly vehicle check process, management do need to incorporate a check of the dashboard light panel and buzzer to ensure driver tampering has not taken place, this process is most important immediately post "switch-on" and until colleagues become accustomed to the new process.

Other Factors to Consider

- Be cognisant that the supplier may try to charge for installation during the negotiation phase. Endeavour to make the supplier absorb this cost, especially if the fleet is 1,000+ or the number of depot locations to install are few and or not remote.
- Avoid paying for the removal of the black box at end of contract. This cost is unnecessary, and the supplier is highly unlikely to spend the time to pay the cost of retrieval of a box that will be several years old, these black boxes have little genuine residue value.
- If the black box fails for any reason (the incidence of failure is likely to be low if fitted correctly), ensure contractually the replacement "new for old" is at the supplier's cost (unless a business employee has tampered or damaged equipment and this can be evidenced) and apply a tight time-limit SLA to achieve replacement. Every day that the black box is not transmitting means zero or inaccurate data and therefore the supplier is preventing the business from generating fuel savings.

In summary, is the introduction of telematics recommended?
Yes. Subject to the caveats outlined above, with the critical factor being that the rental price must be low enough that the net financial position (fuel saving minus rental and other supplier costs) is delivering a minimum return

that the business requires (the minimum return is recommended to be at least 5% excluding additional indirect savings opportunities) and that a pilot, of one large depot which has an experienced team with full buy-in to the project, is conducted as "proof of concept" before committing to a national rollout. In businesses that have not previously installed telematics, savings of 8%–10% are achievable, but only with endeavour and attention to detail and where the supplier will genuinely work in partnership with the business and not abdicate responsibility post installation.

Defect and Accident Reporting

Defect Reporting and Management

Dealing efficiently with vehicle defects and accidents is referenced above as a top ten (point 3) fleet task in association with depot management. It is a legal requirement that vehicles are checked regularly, and management require therefore the driver to complete a daily vehicle check at the start of shift. This process protects the driver, the business, other road users. A generic sample of the vehicle check document is illustrated in Figure 2.3. The document may be a hard copy (paper) or a soft copy and embedded into the PDA function-ality. If the vehicle is not company owned but operated by an "owner-driver" (e.g., Parcel courier) it is best practice to ensure this process is still conducted. Post a serious RTA, possibly involving a fatality, the authorities' (Police and HSE) investigation can be far-reaching, may continue for many months and will absorb significant management time, and may impact business reputa-tion and result in significant fines; therefore, being able to demonstrate robust practices and maintain meticulous records will prove beneficial, and evidence of a completed daily check provides valuable information.

Retaining a record of the check by vehicle registration on a daily basis:

1. Ensures that the business and driver conduct the check.
2. That management have a record to reference should a subsequent prob-lem arise on route or future day that warrants investigation and refer-ence back to a specific date.
3. That vehicle related issues arising from the daily routine are monitored and acted upon to prevent minor issues becoming more significant.

Figure 2.3 is an example of a generic daily driver check sheet. The top sec-tion is standard to all vehicle models and this example includes an ADR

Daily vehicle Check					
Date		Driver			
Reg Plate		Depot			
Tyres				**Lights Operation • Servicable**	
Tyres must have a minimum of 1.6mm tread over ¾ width of tyre				Side & headlights	
	Tread Depth	Visual Pressure	Visual damage	Brake & rear lights	
OSR - Drivers Side Rear				Working Lights in & outside	
OSF - Drivers Side Front				Indicators inc. mirror repeater	
NSF - Passenger Side Front				Reversing	
NSR - Passenger Side Rear				Fog Lights	
Spare Tyre. Servicable and inflated				No Plate light	
				Airside lights	
Interior Van Checks (tick for "yes", X for no)		**Exterior Van Checks**		**Housekeeping**	
Is the cab clean & tidy		Wipers / washers		Fuel Card	
Telematics lightbar operation		Windscreen glass		Defect Book	
Extinguisher secure & in date		Oil- Water - Adblue		Emergency Contact Numbers	
Warning Lights / Messages		Number Plates			
PDA Dock		Exhaust		No Smoking Sign	
Reverse Camera operational		Wheels (damage)		H&S Rules Sticker	
Reversing Sensors operational		Mirrors		Waste Carriers Licence	
Reversing Alarm operational		Side steps		Exterior cleanliness	
Horn		Body Work new defect		MoT & Service in date	
Seats & Seat belts.		Doors & shutters. Operation/locking		Has all accident damage been reported?	
ADR Bag Contents (1 bag per crew member)					
2 ˙ self - standing warning triangles			ADR Instructions (if required) In Writing		
Eye Rinsing Liquid (500ml) in date			Wheel Chock		
Warning Vest			Torch & batteries inserted and ready to use		
Gloves (as required)			Plates (if required) must be undamaged with turnbuttons present and operational		
Protective goggles					
1 X First Aid Kit (Inc 5x 20ml eyes wash vials)			1 X Spill kit		
Driver Comments:					
Manager's signature @ debrief:		Manager comments			
Driver name:		Driver Signature			
Servicable		Defect X		Not Applicable N/A	

Figure 2.3   A sample generic driver daily vehicle check document.

(dangerous good) section. The latter would be altered to reflect the specific vehicle and load being carried. For HGV vehicles, a section for tachograph would be incorporated and additionally any specific elements unique to the vehicle and body design, for example hydraulic lifting equipment, tail lift, side curtains, or shutters, would be incorporated.

Local management must collate all defect sheets to maintain a record by driver and vehicle registration, including a record of the date that defects were resolved. Good practice would be for the depot manager to review progress of all outstanding (unresolved) defects at least on a weekly basis and take requisite action to expedite delays.

Any defect (mechanical, body, or ancillary equipment related) that renders the vehicle un-road-worthy and or unsafe, necessitates the withdrawal of the vehicle immediately from service until the root cause is fixed. Body related defects are as important as engine defects, whether tail lift, shutters, shelves, or "side curtains" related, issues need addressing immediately. Management teams under pressure to get services completed may inadvertently on occasion opt to defer body related repairs, but defective shutters and doors can prove to be the root cause of driver related injuries which may result in the absence at best and industrial claim at worst, and if repeated defect reports have been submitted but not actioned, the business may find itself at the wrong end of an expensive insurance claim. Figure 2.4 provides an example of a generic management defect report which can be used to track defects until resolved, and if applied robustly may mitigate the claim scenario outlined above.

Weekly Vehicle Check

Bringing the defect and maintenance process together is the weekly vehicle inspection that is conducted physically by a member of management together with the primary driver of the vehicle. The 45-point check illustrated in Figure 2.5 is a hard copy, but this can be replicated in a soft copy (Tablet or PDA) and the process should take no more than 10–15 minutes depending on findings.

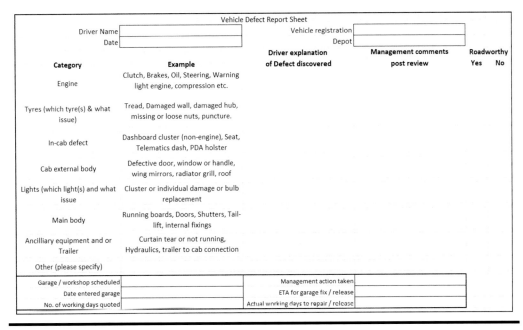

Figure 2.4 Example of a generic management vehicle defect tracking document.

45 point - Weekly vehicle check				
Date		Driver		
Reg Plate		Location		
Tyres				**Lights Operation + Servicable**
1. Tyres must have a minimum of 1.6mm tread over ¾ width of tyre				7. Side & headlights
	Tread Depth	Visual Pressure	Visual damage	8. Brake & rear lights
2. OSR - Drivers Side Rear				9. Work Lights
3. OSF - Drivers Side Front				10. Indicators inc mirror repeater
4. NSF - Passenger Side Front				11.Reversing
5. NSR - Passenger Side Rear				12. Fog Lights
6. Spare Tyre. Servicable and inflated				13. Number Plate lights
				14. Airside lights

Interior Van Checks		**Exterior Van Checks**		**Housekeeping**	
15. Is the cab clean & tidy		25. Wipers / washers		35. Fuel Card (no pin N° displayed)	
16. Telematics instruments working		26. Windscreen/glass		36. Defect Book	
17. Extinguisher secure & in date		27. Oil/Water/Adblu		37. Emergency Contact Numbers	
18. Warning "Dash"		28. Number Plates		(Insurance/Breakdown)	
19. PDA Dock secure		29. Exhaust		38. No Smoking Sign	
20. Reverse Camera operational		30. Wheels (damage)		39. H&S stickers visible	
21. Reversing Sensors operational		31. Mirrors		40. Applicable licence plates	
22. Reversing Alarm audible		32. Side steps		41. Exterior cleanliness	
23. Horn working		33. Body Work		42. MoT & Service in date	
24. Seats/Seat belts. Condition, operation & security		34. Doors, shutters, tail-lift & curtain		43. Has all accident damage been reported?	

Management & Driver sign-off			
Management observations including listing of external damage that is new since last check (PLEASE REFERENCE NUMBER OF ITEM):			
44. Inspected by:	Date.		
45. Drivers Signature:	Date.		
Servicable ✓		Defect ✗	Not Applicable N/A

Figure 2.5   **An example of the weekly 45-point vehicle check.**

Accident Management

Following any vehicle incident/ accident, the business (and specifically local management) needs to gather accurate information and supporting evidence asap in order to:

1. Determine the number and seriousness of any injuries sustained to employees and or third parties, the priority for management is to ensure that colleague injuries and well-being is dealt with appropriately and in serious incidents close relatives notified and duly supported.
2. Investigate and ascertain the root cause. Insurance companies need notifying asap so that they may deal efficiently with third-party insurers which may help reduce third-party costs.
3. Determine if "at-the-scene" attendance by a member of local management or fleet management is required immediately (serious event) or in "slow time" as part of a standard investigative process, but slow time reflects 48 working hours, and it is helpful if the time attending the scene mirrors that of the incident to understand positioning of the sun and other environment factors.

4. Determine how best to recover the vehicle(s) and send on to which repair outlet.
5. To deal appropriately with the employee if fault (post investigation) is apportioned to the driver and by implication.
6. To determine asap if external (e.g. UK logistics or insurance affiliate) independent expertise is required to examine the vehicle and or the scene to provide expert assessment.
7. To understand the root cause and assess whether current company policies or procedures need amending in light of the incident, to help prevent a repeat future occurrence, or whether vehicle design modifications and or additional/different equipment may have provided mitigation.

Figure 2.6 illustrates an example of a generic incident data gathering document (hard or soft copy) required post incident:

Figure 2.6 requires completion at the scene or as soon after the incident and by the driver. Where soft copy completion is not feasible (i.e., via PDA) the company must provide hard copy versions that travel with the vehicle. The driver must be trained on how to complete this document during induction training and prior to being permitted to drive a company vehicle.

As soon as is practical post incident, and whilst at the scene, the driver must contact the company insurance provider and depot management team, the depot team will contact Police if necessary and if not already contacted by either the driver or company insurer. Encourage and train the driver to take as many photographs of the scene using the mobile, including weather conditions and vehicle (company and third parties) conditions possible. If this is not doable for any reason (i.e., due to injury) a member of depot management or nearest driving colleague need to be despatched to the scene without delay.

On the day of the incident (ideally at the scene) and as close in time to the incident as is practical the driver must draw a sketch (Figure 2.7) capturing as much detail as possible, but specifically the road configuration and road markings and approximate position of the company vehicle and other third-party vehicle(s), using arrows to indicate direction of travel. Management must review this diagram as part of the incident investigation (ideally on the same day or within 24 working hours) and discuss in detail and refine the drawing (create a second diagram and retain the original) if more pertinent information can be added that may prove beneficial to insurers and or the police.

Post Accident - Driver information sheet						
Name			**Employee No.**		**No. of years service**	
Address			**Job Title**			
			Date of Birth		**Age**	
			Depot			
			Division			
Have you been involved in an incident in the last 3 years? Provide date and brief description with details of the person at fault						
Have you had a Motoring conviction previously? If yes, please give details including dates and details of outcome						

Incident details				
Location of Incident		**Time of Incident**		
		Date of Incident		
		No. of days absent from work		
Was Incident reported to External Agency?		Report Ref.		Potential Riddor?
Has anyone admitted liability for the Incident? If yes, please provide details				
Description of incident (please provide all relevant details)				

Immediate Actions Taken	
Details of any containement action taken at the time of the incident.	
Details of any Emegency Attendance / Hospital Attendance Provide incident numbers and emergency service provider's details where appropriate	Where possible have the hazards been removed?
	Hazard and hazard triangle in use? (Vehicle Incidents only)
	Driver Check completed for all drivers involved in RTA?
	First Aid Adminstered?

Resulting treatment post Incident	
Type of Treatment Administered	

Figure 2.6   An example of a generic post vehicle accident data capture document.

The incident diagram	
Vehicle Registration	
Details of Damage to Vehicle	
Provide a sketch of the incident Indicating direction of travel of your vehicle, the position of vehicles in the road at time of incident and include any road markings, sign-posts, bollards or traffic lights. Additionally you can provide an annotated google-maps screenshot of the incident. Try to "keep to scale" and add as much detail as you can please. Please state weather conditions, if road wet or dry and the direction from which the sun is shining if the sky is clear. If snowing please state.	

Figure 2.7   A generic "at-the-scene" incident diagram document.

Contact and vehicle details of third parties involved require gathering whilst at the scene (see Figure 2.8), it is also particularly useful to collate witness opinion and contact details.

On the day of the incident (or within 48 working hours) it is good practice to collate basic information regarding the employee(s) and company vehicle involved in the incident and record the points of injury of the colleague involved and areas of damage relating to the commercial vehicle, see Figure 2.9 for reference.

Depot management require training in order to deal effectively with the data collation exercise relevant to Figure 2.9 and give consideration and be sensitive to the colleague who may be under stress if the incident was serious.

At the scene - Eye Witnesses & 3rd Parties			
Record details of other involved parties or witnesses at the scene of the incident; please secure telephone and e-mail contact details, and home or business address. For vehicle incidents ensure that you obtain the car registration make and model and any insurance or legal contact details.			
Witness 1			
Name		Address	
Tel No.			
E-mail Address			
Vehicle Incidents only			
Vehicle Reg.		Car Make and Model	
Insurance Company			
Policy No.			
Witness 2			
Name		Address	
Tel No.			
E-mail Address			
Vehicle Incidents only			

Figure 2.8 An example of a generic "eyewitness and third-party" at-the-scene document.

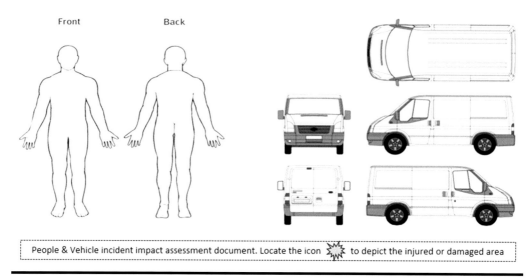

Figure 2.9   An example of incident impact assessment document for the employee and the vehicle.

Period Senior Accident Review

Most serious or fatal injuries are most likely to result from a road traffic incident, such incidents are costly to the business, stressful for involved parties, may impact company reputation, and where a fatality occurs members of management may be involved with various legal bodies and potentially lawsuits for a protracted period of time. Notwithstanding the impact to the business of serious incidents, a multitude of fleet accidents occur with unerring regularity and directly impact business profitability and customer service (VOR trends) and robust measures are required in order to minimise accident trends; to this end, it is good practice to formally review significant accidents at least monthly.

Figure 2.10 illustrates the recommended participants that would attend the fleet accident review. Meetings need not involve every DM every month, depots that are achieving low accident trends with minor incidents deserve recognition rather than be invited to a formal review meeting. The HoF will review all incidents each month and select the DM(s) that need invite to the review based on:

■ A serious accident occurring in the previous month by one or more of the depot driving colleagues, or
■ Where a depot colleague(s) has had two or more incidents/accidents in a rolling 12-month period.

On this basis, experience suggests that a well-constructed presentation compiled by the depot manager (using a company common template) and

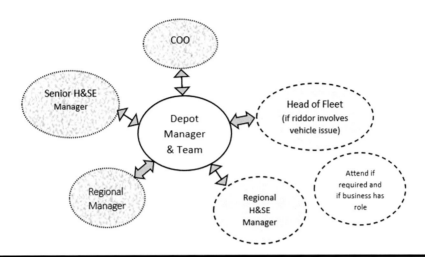

Figure 2.10 Periodic fleet accident review structure.

supported, if necessary, by data supplied by the fleet team should enable an individual depot accident review to be completed in circa 45 minutes unless there is a particularly complex or serious incident requiring discussion. Each month there may be several DMs attending the Accident Review Meeting and the number will define the overall length of the meeting, with each DM invited to attend a specific, and timed, 45-minute segment. The DM will attend with a fully prepared presentation (see below), issued pre-meeting.

The H&S and HR managers play advisory and supporting roles should their guidance be required during the meeting, or they may contribute to follow-up actions post discussion. The two key protagonists are the depot manager and regional operations manager as accountability resides squarely with these roles (specifically the DM) to ensure that accident investigations are conducted quickly, efficiently, and with root causes determined and remedial action taken to prevent future reoccurrence. The presence of the COO may be "light-touch," but attendance demonstrates the importance of the process, and enables authorisation to take any action agreed during discussion, and importantly, where fresh learning is acquired during the review the COO/Operations Director is able to cascade this learning across the wider depot network. Figure 2.11 outlines a suggested five-slide presentation deck that the DM will assemble per driver under review.

Part of the role of the fleet analyst is to provide the COO, HoF, Operations teams, and Finance department with periodic trends on a per depot and business wide basis of the number of incidents and associated cost of damage versus budget, incorporating ratios indicating the average cost per accident per vehicle fleet at the depot level and consolidated by model type nationally.

Slide No.	Who produces & presents	Slide content	Senior team discussion & review aims
1	Depot Manager *(the basics)*	1. Employee name, age, service, disciplinary & absence record, telematics history and trends and traffic offences. 2. Record of previous accidents. When (year & month) & severity. 3. Description of latest incident & associated damaged with costs. 4. Was incident fully investigated to procedure and within 48 hours?	Obtain a rounded view of the driver's (employee) record and attitude and appreciate the history of driving whilst at the company. To ensure the Depot team responded to procedure and investigated immediately and thoroughly.
2	Depot Manager & Fleet Manager *(latest situation)*	1. If serious incident latest update from: 1. Police investigating incident 2. Employee and or third parties injuries 3. Vehicle recovery & repair 4. Affiliate update (i.e. Insurers and independent expert)	If the incident is serious (injuries or fatality) and investigations and repairs on-going, review progress and feedback from all parties. In this circumstance Fleet will provide a latest update from Insurer and any affiliate expert.
3	Depot Manager & Fleet Manager *(root-cause)*	1. Was a 5-why investigative process conducted? 2. What was deemed to be the root-cause(s) and why? 3. Was driver training up to date and all records accurate and current? 4. Was vehicle & equipment in good working order, with servicing & repair records accurate and current? 5. Was driver licence current and legal?	Understand the root cause and determine if localised or having national implications. Has the Depot team maintained records and training accurately and properly. Is there action or further investigation necessary by senior management of the local Depot team?
4	Depot Manager & Fleet Manager *(learnings)*	1. Fleet. Any changes to vehicle model, internal design or fixings required? 2. Fleet. Any changes or alterations required to equipment? 3. Fleet. Any changes in Fleet / company training, policies or procedures? 4. Ops. Were Depot training & daily operating procedures adhered to? 5. Ops. Can Depot or Regional team recommend depot or national changes or improvements, if so what and why?	What are the immediate learnings? Is further work necessary and if so what team(s) should be involved and who lead. Does the Exec team need to be briefed? Is there possible additional expenditure required and why? Have there been any Health & Safety failings and if so where and what? Does the COO need to brief CEO?
5	Depot Manager *(outcome & action taken)*	1. What disciplinary action (if any) was taken against the driver and or any member of the Depot team and why? 2. Were their failings with a garage or within Fleet team, what was it and what action has been taken? 3. Is further discussion and or data required regarding Section 4 (*learnings*) in order to determine improvement solutions and is capex required?	Was action taken reasonable and were any precedents made unwittingly. Does Depot manager and or team need further HR training, is their understanding of employment law and Fleet legislation found wanting? Are there outcome tasks remaining to execute?

Figure 2.11   An accident review presentation template per driver being reviewed. To be completed by the relevant DM and issued to all review participants two days before the scheduled meeting.

Ancillary Devices That Aid Accident Reduction

Reversing sensors (bleepers) are low-cost to install during a new build and highly effective, and many drivers will be used to operating with similar devices in their own private cars. Many damage incidents occur at slow speed when reversing and manoeuvring (depot yards, public carparks, and at customer premises), yet these "soft" incidences can prove to be costly and often involve repair damage of customer or public property. Slow-speed incidents can be potentially dangerous; the elderly or young may be present (school yards, hospital carparks, public carparks, clinics, and doctor surgeries, etc.) and even at low speed, if hit by a reversing van or lorry, the resulting injury can be severe.

Vehicle CCTV. This is recommended at the rear of vehicles to operate in tandem with parking sensors, and for HGV lorries, the recent side elevation CCTV (passenger side specially) provide excellent views of cyclists and pedestrians in busy city centres and country roads.

There are two types of in-cab CCTV, a basic camera looking outward and forward, and an internal CCTV that maintains a watching brief on driver activity. The former is cheap to purchase and install and is recommended, the latter version tend to be expensive, and the author has not found that a business case demonstrates good "value for money." Telematics provides excellent feedback data post incident (indeed impact sensors allow immediate notification to the business at point of impact and in tandem with the dashcam provides sufficient data to review accidents and defend erroneous claims.

Fleet KPIs (Key Performance Indicators)

Without KPIs, it is challenging for a team to measure and monitor performance, track improving trends, and provide data to enable intelligent decision making. However, it is also possible to have KPI "overload" where so many elements are monitored that it is difficult for management to "see the wood for the trees," and it is better to focus on "anchor KPIs" that may significantly enhance performance and profitability, service quality, and employee health and safety. Figure 2.12 illustrates five anchor fleet KPIs.

In order to improve vehicle damage costs and trends, a management team must first understand the root cause of incidents in detail, and to this end, vehicle damage needs to be categorised as illustrated in Figure 2.13.

The monitoring process outlined in Figure 2.13 is best expressed on a per depot, per region, and national basis to enable comparative analysis between depots. As more data is gathered it will become feasible to measure current vs. previous year (for the same month) to appreciate trend improvement.

The guideline table in Figure 2.12 provides five fleet "anchor" KPIs that are particularly useful to fleet and operational management to aid decision making and provide early warning of diminished performance and or a lack of management focus at the depot. These five KPIs should be incorporated into the budget planning process so that a target is set for each KPI for each DM by month, and once the new budget year commences, each month Fleet and Finance will produce monthly reporting documents indicating for each KPI actual vs. budget (and variance).

Fleet: Challenging "Perceived Wisdom"

Businesses must continually evolve and introduce new techniques and methodologies with the objective of maintaining or improving service quality,

Anchor Fleet KPIs. *Examples assume a total Fleet number of 1,000. VOR reflects "vehicle off road."*					
The KPI	The measurement	The Calculation	D	W	M
Fleet uptime @ 96%	The % of VOR, expressed as "uptime" with a target of 96% or higher, this target is applicable for all Fleets irrespective of size or type.	Number of VOR vehicle days over the total Fleet number multiplied by the number of working days in the period (month). Example, VOR for a Monday is 32, therefore 32/1,000 * 100 = 3.2%, uptime equalling 96.8%. The weekly VOR was 182; therefore 182 / (5*1,000) *100 = 3.6%, weekly uptime is 96.4%	✓	✓	✓
72-hour report @ 15% or VOR	Number of VOR remaining in garage (or workshop) for longer than 3 working days. Target <15% of VOR.	This measure maintains pace on in-house workshops and or external servicing and repair garages. The KPI excludes long-term accident damage or bodywork repairs. In the example above weekly VOR was 182, so the target would be more than 27 (15%) of VORs in garage for longer than 3 working days, with the garage(s) required to provide a daily report listing Reg for every vehicle +3 days with an explanation and target return to Depot date. This KPI should form part of the suppliers contractual SLA		✓	✓
Speeding incidences, target 0.75 per driver day	Where Telematics is installed, the management target is to achieve 0.75 instances of speeding per driver per day on average.	The measure is calculated on actual driver days. In the example there are 920 drivers on the road (excluding holidays & absence) on Monday, therefore the target is 690 instances (0.75 over 920), and any driver with +1 instances will need formal review during Driver debrief.	✓	✓	✓
Vehicle accident damage ratios	1.The number of vehicle accidents per depot expressed as a ratio of total depot Fleet. 2. The average cost per accident (per depot) 3. The number of drivers that have had 1+ accidents during a rolling thirteen month period.	Each business will set the target. These KPIs are intended to measure trends per depot and driver and are designed to improve performance over time whilst highlighting specific drivers that require either further training or formal review if there driving is sub-standard. Applying RAG indicators and producing league tables per depot and driver will add focus to improving what can be a high-cost line and debilitating to Fleet and subsequent customer service.		✓	✓
No. of and £ of Hire per day	The Finance Dept. to produce actual cost of, and number of vehicle hire days per depot, region and nationally.	The number and cost of hires should be incorporated in a budget where hires are used to supplement peak / seasonal trading, but hires may supplement in-year organic or new business growth, otherwise hire numbers should be theoretically zero if the Fleet is well maintained and accident ratios as expected and the 72-hour KPI is expediting vehicle return from repair. Depots may be prone to "holding-on" to hires longer than is necessary as a safety net. Measure trends, implement at least regional authorisation enabling hire expenditure and investigate every hire at depot each month to ensure the necessity of hire.		✓	✓
Note: D = Daily, W = Weekly and M = Monthly					

Figure 2.12   Anchor fleet KPIs suitable for most fleet types and sizes.

reduce costs, improve driver and other colleagues or public safety, reduce accidents, or increase load capacity. The "new" technique may be genuinely innovative, or a tried and tested concept deployed in other businesses but not yet deployed in the business you work for. It is commonplace for managers to become comfortable with processes and procedures that exist in the business, and which are perceived as good practice and have been successfully deployed for many years, the "we have always done it this way"

Accident category	Period totals	Year to date	YTD previous year	Forecast target
Reversing or Parking				
Hit Stationary Object				
Vehicle mirror damage				
Hit another Parked Vehicle				
Vehicle Hit Whilst Parked / Unnoticed				
Alleged Accident				
Hit Rear of Third Party				
Other / miscellaneous				
Roundaboutor Junction Collision				
Actual / attempted theft or vandalism				
Overtaking or "Passing" incident				
Collision with vulnerable Road User				
Narrow Road Collision				
Total accidents				
Total accidents as a ratio over total Fleet				

Figure 2.13   Sub-categorisation of vehicle damage KPI.

syndrome. But if companies are to avoid stagnating operationally and prevent competitors from becoming more efficient, management teams need to remain open-minded to new different ideas and concepts, whether initiated from existing colleagues or new incoming employees. Two areas of opportunity which the author has found to be commonly overlooked operationally, but which offer significant profit potential is the concept of "double-shifting" vehicles, and creation of an in-house fleet design team (these are not dedicated roles but a coming together of minds) to enhance future vehicle design.

Double-Shifting

Many logistics businesses operate their fleet across a small proportion of the 24-hour clock, too often the fleet (reflecting the most expensive physical asset in the business) will have "wheels-turning" for no more than nine to ten hours each day (38%–42% of the full day) and some companies operate smaller windows and further compound this inactivity with a five-day working week resulting in a weekly utilisation of only 29%.

"Double-shifting" is the term used when a vehicle is used more than once (by more than one driver) in a 24-hour period. The vehicle will complete one shift, return to depot to be off-loaded, inspected, and re-fuelled to then operate a second shift which may be a part or full shift. Any double-shifting will deliver an increase in utilisation and a reduction in fleet (the total num-ber of vehicles in the fleet) and this will increase profit. It is incumbent on the management team to continually review opportunities that may arise with growth, but this may require support and understanding of other departments, for example Sales and Marketing, in order, for example to facilitate a widening (extending) of customer opening hours regarding access to service (which may be different from the customer's standard "open-ing hours"), this may involve customers being receptive to changes in their modus operandi, or enabling access via a third-party cleaning or guarding supplier, but worthy of consideration if there is a genuine commercial incen-tive for both parties.

Any extension to a standard (8–9 customer hour window) operating win-dow for a proportion of the customer base can provide genuine opportunity. For example:

1. Can the customer's operating window be extended from say eight/nine hours per day to 12? This modest extension would enable a reduc-tion in the number of days the business may operate (from a five- to a four-day week) and increase work-day asset utilisation to 50%, allow-ing a full working day for servicing and inspection at day-rate pricing. Some customers will already have availability to service out of hours, they simply need identifying, the business historically has simply slotted their drop times into the standard operating window for convenience. Extending to 12 may enable part-time staff to operate a part-shift.
2. It is highly unlikely that double-shifting will apply to more than c40% of the existing fleet, but even if sufficient clusters of customers can change to enable just 10%–20% of double-shifting in city depots, the savings to the business will be significant. Operations and Sales should formulate a target plan to concentrate on city-based customer locations regarding out-of-hours access, stem mileages will be reduced, and drop density greater which will render the second route more productive.
3. Alternatively, is it feasible that the working week can be extended from five to six or seven days? What percentage of customers currently, or in the future could open longer?

Where double-shifting is feasible (even if in part, geographically defined or limited to specific customers) the larger the vehicle (HGV) and more expensive the vehicle, the better the savings to the business will be. Driver costs are unlikely to be reduced when introducing double-shifting, indeed they may increase if the second shift operated warrants a premium for unsocial hours, but this may be partially offset by a reduction in previous overtime trends. Whilst vehicle maintenance costs per mile will increase as the asset is working harder for longer, where the author has successfully introduced double-shifting in businesses that have operated historically a single shift, the bottom-line savings to the business have proved material, sustainable, and provided more flexibility and opportunities for the sales teams.

Whilst the Executive team, Sales and Finance will welcome a profit enhancement opportunity, be under no illusion that a minority of depot managers and their teams may resist change. Double-shifting may require depot management teams to operate the depot for longer hours, cover additional days, and shift patterns for the depot team may require to be introduced. Delivering change is rarely a simple task, it requires hard work, high energy a change to the status quo, but delivering change can be exciting and rewarding. Introducing change is a core managerial responsibility, businesses won't evolve and improve without change, reticent managers should ask themselves, "if this was my business, and I owned 100% of the company shares would I want to initiate the change to maximise profit and business growth?" If the answer is yes, then buckle-up and support the change programme.

Enhanced Vehicle Design

A creative and technically proficient fleet team working collaboratively with an innovative senior operations team will have the wherewithal and desire to reduce costs and improve driver colleagues' working environment through continual evolution of vehicle design.

▪ *Retaining the fundamental design but change build materials.*
   Savings may be modest but by using lighter build materials and challenging perceived wisdom iterative change is possible, for example: reducing the fuel tank size/capacity (urban only), removing unnecessary doors and replacing with lightweight panels, removing the passenger seat (if not needed and replace with a storage box), new build vehicle pricing can be reduced without detriment to the basic operating mode of the vehicle, and lightening the GVW delivers either better fuel consumption and or greater carrying capacity (weight) if the chassis remains unchanged.

■ *Body design change.*

Each vehicle model type has a maximum load capacity depending on the type of load carried, and typically the constrain will be either:

– *Cubic capacity.* The load area cannot physically fit anymore product inside due to lack of space.

– *Weight capacity.* The maximum legal weight permitted for transportation is achieved whilst cubic capacity exists.

– *Insurance capacity.* There is surplus weight and or cubic capacity available, but the vehicle's cargo has reached the insurance capacity (for example, precious cargo or Cash in Transit – CIT).

Management teams must adopt a "first principles" review of vehicle design to understand if and what modifications can be made to enhance relevant capacity. It is often cost prohibitive to refurbish existing vehicles' part way through its life, and more productive to focus on introducing change to new vehicles. Below are actual examples of changes that were successfully introduced, all of which increased profitability through reduced costs and improved drops per route which in turn reduced overall fleet numbers.

Cubic and Weight Capacity

The cab remained unchanged, but a chassis was found that enabled the rear converted body to be situated nearer to the ground enabling an overall increase in the body height and in tandem with a redesigned body the cubic capacity was increased by c15%. Additional shelving was incorporated, the rear doors were removed, and lightweight side-sliding doors replaced conventional heavy steal shutters. Employee accidents reduced due to decreased back and shoulder strains (worn shutters) and less stretching and reaching as a result of lowering the body nearer to the ground.

Weight Capacity

A transformational business change in customer product design coupled with a simpler, smaller customer installation methodology resulted in the fleet being able to operate a smaller chassis vehicle, and the introduction of this vehicle included a redesigned storage compartment with compartment dimensions specifically modelled to snuggly house driver equipment, consumables, and product. The result delivered a new vehicle type that was two times (overall dimension) smaller than the previous model. Not only was the purchase price significantly reduced, but the miles per gallon (mpg) was improved by c30%.

Insurance and Weight Capacity

The UK historically (1990–2010) experienced the highest number of "across-the-pavement" attacks on CIT drivers as a ratio to vehicles of any country in the world. CIT crew would often include two employees, one remaining in the vehicle and one transporting cash by foot "across-the-pavement." However, this modus operandi enabled criminals to "duress" the internal crewmember by physically threatening the external member. Following a collaborative exercise with stakeholders including manufactures, design engineers, union, employees, fleet team, and operational management, a full-proof biometric one-person entry system was designed to render it impossible for two individuals (no matter what their size) to fit in a new vehicle airlock (double-door access module) entrance simultaneously. This enhancement:

■ Reduced a two-person operation to one,
■ Saved c80 kgs of weight (average person's weight) enhancing vehicle weight capacity,
■ Reduced duress attacks significantly, improving attack absence and employee safety,
■ Enabled an increase in the carrying cash and associated insurance limit.

Electric vs. Hydrogen Engine

Logistical businesses are busy evaluating the benefits of transitioning from diesel (combustion engine) to electric vehicles with some companies generating perceived marketing kudos from early introduction, although for some businesses this is in practice a token number of electric vehicles (EVs) providing a semblance of being "greener" and more sustainable.

Whilst the government has issued targets for cars and vans to transition to "zero emissions" by 2035, offering grants for "plug-ins" (workplace charger scheme) and commercial electric vehicle grants; the UK charging infrastructure is embryonic and electric vehicles remain very expensive (relative to current combustion equivalents) and most have inhibiting mileage range suitable in practice only for inner city environments, and the ability of doing this in turn relies on the business city depots having an electricity supply capability able to support new generation electric vehicles, which is not straightforward and which may add significantly to the cost of introduction.

EVs are powered via lithium-ion batteries, and the residue waste from EVs presents an entirely new waste stream for businesses and governments to grapple with that will become of epic proportion and which arguably has not yet been fully considered, and not yet resolved. Just six companies produce c85% of batteries for cars in 2020 and the material is sourced from largely from South America, the author understands this material cannot be widely sourced geographically around the world. In the race to move from combustion to EV have the longer-term impacts been extensively researched and thought through?[1]

FCVs (fuel cell vehicles) are fuelled by hydrogen and whilst this concept is a "late-starter" compared to EV, the concept continues to gain ground. The pros include much faster refuelling times (10 minutes versus 30–40 with EV), potentially longer drive time, and zero emissions from FCV other than harmless warm water vapour. The cons are that despite being ubiquitously present hydrogen needs splitting from combined molecules such as water (H_2O) and herein lies the problem as the most common methodologies use fossil fuels which is counter-productive to reducing emissions. However, there are many exciting prototypes in evidence across the world[2] including AlGalCo. (India) that have a "hydrogen on-tap" principle be trialled with buses in the City of Carmel, and which is approved by the Environment Protection Agency, this concept uses water dripped onto aluminium and gallium cylinders to produce on-the-spot hydrogen.

Hyundai has introduced hydrogen trucks in Switzerland leased via Hyundai Hydrogen Mobility. Shell is developing a hydrogen infrastructure in the UK for commercial vehicles, and vehicle converters ULEMCo – in conjunction with Revolve Technologies – are claiming record efficiency results. Whilst hydrogen conversion is expensive Lancaster University research team can visualise improving trends as volume demand increases over time. JCB announced in October 2021[3] a billion-pound purchase deal of green hydrogen from Forlescue Future Industries in order to distribute across the UK via Ryze Hydrogen.

Will there emerge therefore a "two-horse" race to supply an alternative to the standard combustion engine during the next decade?

The next decade will bring much innovation and technological advancement and in 2022 it is arguably too early to unequivocally endorse either EV or FCV as being the right "horse-to-back" and current offerings remain cost prohibitive with refuelling infrastructures that are wholly inadequate, and as the market continues to advance rapidly the author's view is that businesses must continue to keep abreast of research initiatives whilst conducting modest and targeted pilots with no more than a handful of, in city environments, to better understand practical considerations. For the next three to five years, it is prudent to quell the over-enthusiastic fleet manager who may advocate going-green prematurely, but each year re-evaluate the science and latest innovations together with a detailed understanding of both electric and hydrogen refuelling infrastructures for commercial vehicles, and let other businesses sacrifice profit in their desire to be guinea pigs. There is no immediate imperative to determine a definitive strategy and patience will save money, and in view of the life expectancy of a commercial vehicle (4–10 years), investing prematurely in embryonic model variants may prove unnecessarily costly and less efficient.

Vehicle Replacement

Vehicles are either purchased outright by the company (capex) and depreciated across the life of the vehicle or leased and the latter will normally include a fixed replacement term and penalty clauses (increased pence-per mileage charges and or overall maintenance cost increases) if the agreed term is extended by mutual agreement.

The normal term for a small van or car-derived van is four to five years depending on the expected average annual mileage and this may be influenced by whether the vehicle operates one or more "shifts" (a shift could range between c8–12 hours in duration) each day and the number of days per week the vehicle will operate. Lease companies may increase R&M charges if the vehicle is operating continually in dense city centres as some parts (clutch, brakes) may wear faster than in rural use.

When leasing, it is recommended that mileage is "pooled" and aggregated across the full fleet to avoid paying excess mileage for a limited number of vehicles that may exceed expected mileage. Avoid paying premiums for city-based vehicles. The fleet management team should maintain weekly and periodic mileages per vehicle to track progress and if certain vehicles are become excessively high, these can be "shuffled" with low-mileage vehicles. This "levelling" process will help avoid unnecessary R&M, wear and tear costs, and also prolong tyre life across the fleet.

When purchasing direct via capex, the cost of the vehicle is "depreciated" in financial terms across the expected life of the vehicle, the depreciation process enables the business to plan and provide for procurement of new vehicles at end of life. There are a range of factors that influence the expected lifespan of a vehicle:

1. GVW. Broadly small vans 4–5 years, large vans 7–8, and HGV 8–10 years. Note: Trailers are depreciated over a much longer period, 15–20 years, with a body refurbishment planned and budget for at half-life. The half-life principle may also apply to vehicles where either the body or engine is expected to wear sooner than the other. For example, in the CIT sector, the body has extensive and expensive modifications to the rear and cab to render the vehicle secure and therefore a planned half-life new engine block combined with a modest body "refresh" is widespread practice to extend chassis life to 12–14 years.
2. Miles driven annually. This may be influenced by the number of shifts (journeys per 24 hours) and days per week the vehicle works. Note, a "shift" is assumed to be in the range of 8–12 hours duration.
3. The geography in which the vehicle is operated. Urban city usage will be harder wearing on clutches and brakes and smaller city roads and tight access gates/entrances combined with old, congested yards may impact external damage trends.
4. The environment. Off-road working for example (e.g. construction sites, landfill sites) will be less forgiving than motorway miles.
5. High employee attrition or environments in which a vehicle has multiple drivers are likely to incur higher incident/accident rates and clutch changes as these vehicles will be "less-loved" than one where a driver and vehicle are able to be broadly twinned for extended periods.

The benefit of direct purchase is that the business has full control of the fleet assets and greater flexibility regarding the procurement cycle. With good management, it may be possible to extend the operating life of a vehicle beyond its depreciated life without detriment to service, and in this instance the business has a depreciation "saving" (once depreciated the "book value" of the vehicle is zero) and planned cash outlay is deferred until it is necessary to replace new for old.

It is important that excessive numbers of vehicles are not purchased and introduced to the business in a single year, as they will fully depreciate collectively and cause spiking procurement cycle within the procurement cycle.

If the expected lifespan for the fleet is say eight years (see Figure 2.14), ideally the business would be planning to renew c12.5% of fleet vehicles annually to maintain a smooth procurement and investment programme. Where a cycle has become unbalanced the Head of Fleet, COO, and the Finance dept. need to collaborate to produce a coherent plan that will rebalance the cycle across a number of years through extending a proportion of end-of-life vehicles (those with less mileage and lowest annual R&M costs), and thinning the planned new vehicles as far as is practical into future years.

For example, if the business has c100 vehicles (Figure 2.14) and all are expected to last c8 years, ideally each year the business is procuring 12–13 vehicles (12.5%). This helps minimise cash outlay each year and allows the business to be more fluid in reacting to volume changes in the business, changes in legislation, and customer requirements. For example, if business loses 50% of revenue (or a single but material contract) and the associated services (drops) plummet over a relatively brief period (such instances occur regrettably) but the previous year the business replaced 60% of its fleet, the business may be burdened with excessive and unwanted costs.

Another benefit of a smooth replacement programme is that vehicle evolution and design changes can be incrementally introduced. Conversely, the fiscal impact associated with a large contract loss can be softened as the business is able to "right-size" by placing annual procurement programmes

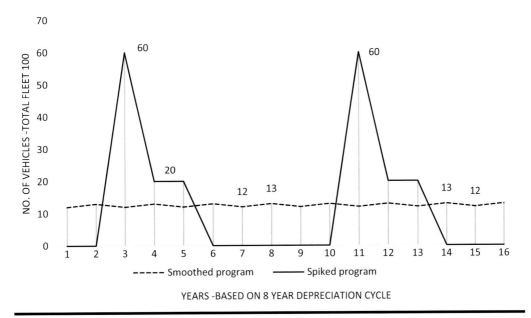

Figure 2.14   Fleet procurement cycles.

on hold. Once purchased direct (or leased), it is costly to terminate a vehicle mid-life. Regarding the advent of EV/FCV vehicles in future years and the unpredictability of the market and embryonic nature of the vehicles, it would be prudent to avoid investing in large numbers of these vehicles until the business is confident that they are entirely suitable and will withstand the test of time.

Fuel Management

Depots with HGV fleet predominantly use bunkered fuel (for an example of a bunker[4]) in contrast to businesses deploying LCVs which predominantly use garage fuel cards. HGV trucks have fuel tanks with capacities in the range of 400–600 litres and therefore refuelling at bunkers within the depot network is more practical, saves redundant refuelling mileage, and bunded fuel is significantly cheaper than garage fuel because bulk delivered.

Bunds produce electronic reports that record the usage by driver and or registration (usually activated by a unique keypad code or driver fob) that provide excellent consumption data for management.

Commercial van businesses predominantly use garage forecourt fuel cards which can be used on-the-go and at any time, and as all the major fuel retailers (e.g. Shell and BP) have strong national coverage, a vehicle is therefore never too far from a petrol station. However, the fuel card user is not "captive" to a dedicated fuelling station in the way the HGV driver tends to be; the refuelling process is easy, but the fuel card is associated with the vehicle registration not the driver, and in large fleets, this may render tracking of spend by driver more problematic unless a strict control mechanism is implemented, or driver and vehicle remain broadly linked together. Data reports and useful KPIs from the large fuel retailers are not always easy reads and may therefore require the fleet management team to apply secondary analysis in order to identify usage trends and pinpoint erroneous individual driver usage which may indicate theft.

To aid control, management should seek exception reports from the card provider that produce summary statistical data indicating:

- Vehicles that fuel twice in any given day.
- Vehicles that fuel more often than the average weekly usage trend. If a vehicle refuels on average three times, investigate 4+ refuelling incidences.

- Check every weekend or out-of-hours refuelling to validate if driver was actually "at-work."

Analysis of usage by vehicle model type is useful in determining average consumption (miles per gallon or litre) within the model category, split urban and rural, and this may provide foundation data which the fleet team can and investigate vehicles at the high usage "end" and may provide early signs of mechanical problems and or identify driver misuse worthy of further research.

Notes

1. Risky business: The hidden costs of EV battery raw materials. 23 November 2020. Nathan Picarsic. Automotive World.
2. Commercial Motor. 21 October 2019. A closer look at the hydrogen fuelled truck. https://www.commercialmotor.comJeff Brown. 16 October 2020. Are Hydrogen Fuel Cells better than Lithium-ion Batteries? https://www.brownston-eresearch.com
3. Katy Austin. BBC News. 31 October 2021. JCB signs green hydrogen deal worth billions. https://www.bbc.co.uk
4. contact@metcraft.co.uk. sales@fueltankshop.co.uk

Chapter 3

Route Scheduling

Introduction

Route scheduling is at the core of any route-based logistics business. It encompasses the methodology of planning a vehicle route with the aim to optimise the number of drops (sometimes referred to as service visits or stops) completed per hour and per route (journey, working day). This practice is a science not an "art." Scheduling practitioners may be referred to as either "planners" or "schedulers."

Without a formal, structured scheduling process conducted by trained scheduling practitioners, any route-based business is almost certainly going to operate sub-optimally with the result that operating costs will be unnecessarily high and productivity (drops per route) too low. In any operation over a period of a just few months, depots will have new customer drops added to the drop pool, and lost customer work and associated drops will be lost from the pool, the mix of drops across a depot's servicing geography is fluid and changing literally on a weekly basis, and this phenomenon is further influenced by seasonal volume fluctuations (Christmas, Easter, school and summer holiday) and other environmental factors (road closures, building works, inclement weather). This ever-changing landscape is challenging for schedulers, and all routes will quickly become sub-optimal unless the disciplines regarding route scheduling absolutely robust, structured, and procedures consistently applied by trained practitioners. Further, inconsistencies will emerge in just a couple of months if scheduling data (customer addresses, contractual service conditions, etc.) is not current and accurate. Figures 3.1 and 3.2 illustrate an example of the "before" and "after"

DOI: 10.4324/9781003323822-3

impact (the examples reflect a fictitious Reading (Berkshire) depot, and each example illustrates the same day of the week) following the introduction of either a software scheduling program with a trained practitioner where none has previously existed, or a first-principles scheduling "refresh" of unkempt routes is completed manually by an experienced route scheduling team.

Incorporating a periodic (at least quarterly) formal review of all routes at a depot is good practice, this will ensure that the impact of customer gains and losses is controlled to prevent significant degradation of route productivity. When analysing a depot's drop pool, it is important to assess the inter-depot boundary areas of neighbouring depots to ensure that outlying drops in close proximity to boundaries are aligned to the most appropriate depot, these may change overtime, and therefore, a holistic approach incorporating clusters of depots during a periodic review will best optimise productivity. In Figure 3.1, the depot at Reading has a neighbouring depot at Bristol (Southwest) and which services Newbury (ringed left), Reading is geographically closer and stem mileage (between depot location and service area) is

Figure 3.1   An example of the service drops on one day from a depot located in Reading (Berkshire), before route scheduling principles have been introduced. Note: view in tandem with Figure 3.3.

significantly less from Reading than from Bristol, an example of a boundary line change. The other two ringed drop zones (red coloured drop – top right and amber coloured bottom left) indicate recently won customers added to the drop pool. These drops were initially allocated to Reading depot, but the Guildford new service was incorrectly added to the amber route (see Figure 3.2), but the neighbouring depot already has a vehicle servicing this specific geography.

Figure 3.2 illustrates the "after" picture post route "cleansing." Unnecessary cross-over of drops, where vehicles from two routes attend the same town on the same day, has been eliminated and the routes are visibly more logical and as a consequence the overall miles travelled for the five vehicles on the sample day is reduced and therefore more efficient and less costly.

These routes all have drops close to the depot; this configuration will be more prevalent in city depots where drop density is greater; rural depots are likely to reflect a higher average mileage from depot to first drop and reflect a lower drops per mile than city depots. Some route scheduling software

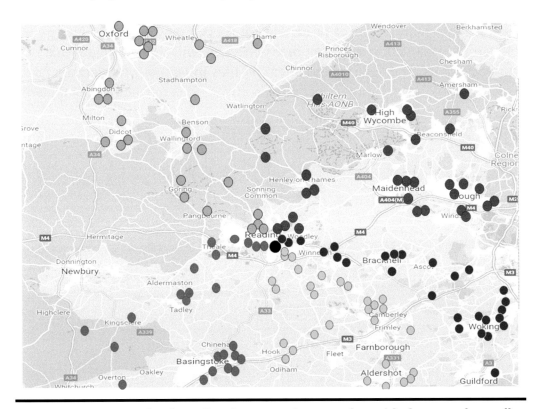

Figure 3.2   An example of Reading depot, on the same day, with the same drops allocated to routes post a routing and scheduling exercise to eradicate waste and enhance productivity.

packages favour a "lollipop" concept, which is broadly a loop outwards from the depot, and continuing to loop geographically around until returning to the depot, other methods favour long stem mileage driving to the furthest point (before rush-hour traffic impedes average speed) and working logically backwards to the depot. The distance between the depot and the first drop of the route, and from the last drop back to the depot is known as "stem mileage," see Figure 3.3. Mileage between clusters of drops is called "radial mileage."

In principle, stem mileage should be as short as is feasible, both on the outward and return journey to the depot, with radial mileage, the distance between each drop as small as possible. Productive time occurs when the driver and the vehicle is at the customer location (drop time), this period of time is when revenue is being generated (the business is charging the customer for the service being performed), travel time is non-revenue earning but a necessary "enabler" to providing the service, so the target is the shortest travel time possible and maximum drop(s) and drop time. Where route planning is sub-optimal (for whatever reason), introducing either a skilled practitioner to manually plan or implement specialised route-scheduling software in conjunction with a trained scheduler will achieve significant efficiency gains. The "before and after" profiles in Figure 3.4 reflect an actual example where route scheduling software was introduced combined

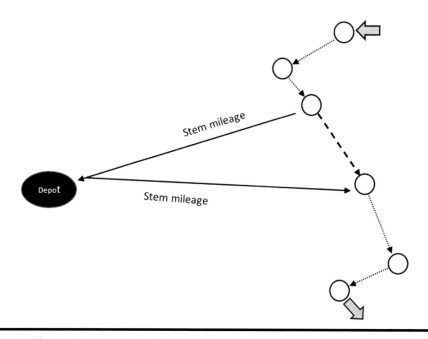

Figure 3.3   Illustrating "stem" mileage.

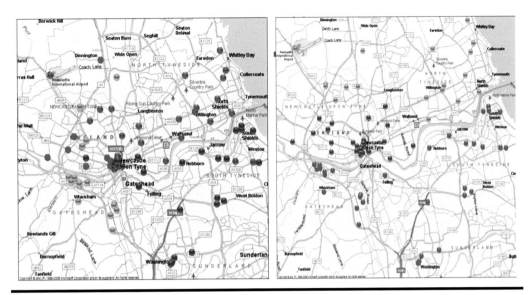

Figure 3.4 **An illustration of the "before and after" positive impact of applying route scheduling software in tandem with a trained practitioner. This actual example was a Newcastle depot where five routes were reduced to three.**

with a skilled planning practitioner resulting in five routes being trimmed to three representing a 40% reduction; and whilst this gain may appear high, it illustrates the deterioration that creeps into depots' routing due to the ever-changing landscape of gained and lost drops, combined with untrained or incompetent personnel left to "route plan" in an unstructured environment, the up-side potential should not be underestimated.

The solution (Figure 3.4) involved concentrating all close proximity drops nearest to the depot into a single route to provide an inner-city high-density route, with the two "outlying" routes planned in "lollipop" fashion with drops planned on the outward and inward journeys to reduce the non-productive stem mileage.

There are many variables that influence route planning, these are illustrated in Figure 3.5.

Organisational Design

There are broadly two scheduling personnel structures, one that deploys a dedicated planner or planning team in each depot (dependent on number of operating routes requiring planning), and the second reflect a planning team(s) which is consolidated into a single national team or a limited

Variable	Impact on scheduling function
Customer opening times, days of opening number of visits required per week.	Fixed times and or days inhibit drops-per-day productivity. If multiple visits per week are required (excluding the everydayvisits) productivity is improved if the actual day of visit is not fixed. E.g. if 2 visits per week are required attempt to establish a 1-or 2-day gap between visits rather thanapply a fixed day. If specific windows are required within the day negotiate the widest possible window, every hour negatively impacts drop productivity, seek AM or PM (4-hour window) as a minimum if feasible.
Length of working day	Businesses usually collect, deliver or work at customer premises when they are open. Seek to lengthen the day as long as possible. Some customers have security or cleaning staff on site during out-of-hours, and this may be sufficient in order to allow the supplier to gain access.
Depot opening restrictions	Depots in city centres may have operatingtime restrictions and or noise restrictions if the immediate vicinity is housing estate and not industrial
The actual time at customerlocation	This is a key variable. It is important therefore that regular (at least annually) analysis is conducted by operational management to accurately measure the time on site per unit (E.g. number of stillages, parcels, products,or installation / processing or servicing time per working unit). Measure average walk time in / out and appreciate specific location factors ("x" flights of stairs, restricted access times, height, or weight limitations for vehicles) all need factoring into the routing program, and crucially the business customer database must be current with accurate data(including but not limited to, address, postcodewindow time, special instructions, contact detailsetc.).If the time-on site is not accurate it may inhibit route productivity. THIS IS A KEY VARIABLE.
Fleet variables	If there are varying Fleet models (vehicle variants) operating at the same depot with different configuration and capacities (weight, height, width, on-board equipment such as mechanical lifting equipment) the scheduling program must contain accurate data, obviously the more vehicle variants with unique specification are likely toinhibit scheduling flexibility
Driver variables	Drivers may need legal (E.g. ADR certification, driving licence) or specific customer training (on-site, with product or security certification) and this driver "skill matrix" data must be accurate and current.
Order "cut-off" time & ad-hoc orders	The cut-off time of day that final orders are received (for next day delivery) is critical as this timing impacts the scheduling operation, a route cannot be finalised until all drop data is input(which may be required during the evening), and late cut-off times will influence any associated packing and loading times. If ad-hocorders apply (received today for delivery today –"same day") this will greatly inhibit drops per driver day and somebusinesses deploy a secondary operational solution if ad-hoc volume is low, but important, to avoid impacting the majority of routes.
Advance booking to access	If customers require advance booking with a location to agree a time and day / date (e.g. Prisons, Schools, Hospitals) this adds an additional layer of complexity for the business as the process will need completing before scheduling takes place to incorporate the drop, or it is treated as a "special" rather like ad-hoc, but this will inhibit output.
SLA service level agreement	Each business will agree with each customers a contractual SLA. Excluding force-majeure, missed services, or partially completed services will be "targeted" as a percentage with failure perhaps incurring a financial penalty (credit). The range "on-time" contractual service is usually in therange 95-98%. Every one-percent requirement will represent a significant cost (number of drivers and vehicles) implication to the business, and it is important therefore to set thecontractual SLA as low as is acceptable on a per customer basis, applying a blanket high business level percentage is unnecessary and will come with a price.

Figure 3.5   Contractual and operational variables that may inhibit scheduling productivity.

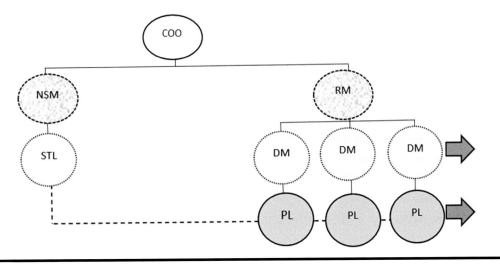

Figure 3.6   The "planner per depot" model.

number of regional planning teams. There are pros and cons attributable to each methodology. Figure 3.6 illustrates the planner-per-depot model. To aid orientation to both example schematics, the icon initials reflect the following management role:

COO	Chief Operating Officer (Ops Director)	RM	Regional Ops Manager/Director
NSM	National Scheduling Manager	DM	Depot Manager
STL	Scheduling Team Leader	PL	Planner (individual scheduler)

The number of STL roles depend on the number of Depots but a ratio of 1:6 (STL to PL) is recommended as a guide. The central scheduling functional support team led by the NSM will be small in this model as their role is strategic, involving holistic modelling and the team is outward facing with third-party scheduling software supplier(s). Training of the planner (scheduler) will be conducted by the STL. The direct-line (hard-line) management line responsibility of the PL resides with the DM situated in the depot where the planner resides. If depots have less than 20 vehicles one planner may span two depots and assume responsibility for planning routes at both.

With this model, there is likely to be less direct collaboration between the individual planners in different depots, and it is more challenging to ensure commonality of training and uniformity of the scheduling techniques deployed by each planner; indeed, "creep" of poor practice and deviation from company scheduling protocols is less easy to detect and control in this model as the planner reports to and influenced strongly by the DM. A common rationale used to promote this model is that the local planner has "local" geographical knowledge that aids optimal scheduling. This view may have relevance in large city environments including London, Manchester, and Birmingham but only if the planner's road-map knowledge is extensive with genuine depth, but in practice a local planner will add little to the finessing of scheduled routes due to his or her geographical expertise. This "urban myth" gives no credence to the extensive algorithm "engines" that modern route scheduling software packages incorporate, and which cope with city scheduling with relative ease. Whilst a local planner does interface with drivers directly and is able to "listen-in" during debrief and is more readily able to receive direct driver feedback regarding customer location challenges (e.g. insufficient time per location, wrong address details, specific location detail such as stairs), all of which may constructive, the local management team members (not the planner) need to receive and action such data change requests. The planner may also be unduly influenced by drivers that are work colleagues, perhaps friends or strong influential personalities able to persuasively argue their case to relax standards whether the data they present is factually correct or not. This model requires the DM to be knowledgeable about route scheduling and company processes and be fully supportive of the planner and the role and to ensure that a healthy, productive working environment is established and maintained at the depot, and is one in which the planner can focus entirely on the job of optimising routes without undue and negative influence.

Figure 3.7 illustrates the centrally based model of planners, situated in one or more locations, these planning teams route schedule independently and do not reside in the local geography. The benefits of this model are that uniformity of procedures and scheduling processes are easier to ensure and control due to having a "captive audience," and training is more straightforward, coherent, and less costly to administer. Additionally, holiday/absence and attrition-related "cover" is more readily achieved.

The negative aspect of this model is that depot operations and some DMs may seek to divorce themselves from being accountable for and owning optimised route scheduling as an objective of the role, seeing it as someone else's responsibility. To counter this fallacy, senior operational management actively promote the model and ensure unequivocal local management buy-in. Centralised scheduling is perceived as more "remote" regarding planner–driver and planner–DM collaboration, and this countering with a robust

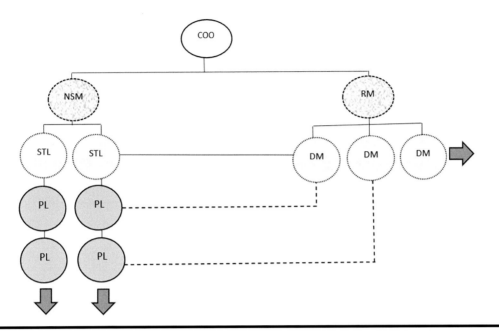

Figure 3.7   The central scheduling model.

operational drumbeat (see Chapter 9, "Operating Rhythm (Drumbeat)") to incorporate the following operational disciplines:

■ Once routes are fully completed (including the finessing process) by planners, they are formally shared, reviewed, and agreed as being optimal and "fit-for-purpose" with the DM before being declared as completed.

■ Routes are "pre-briefed" by local depot management teams with drivers the day before the route commences, to avoid any reasons why a drop(s) "cannot-be-done." Once this process is complete, 100% route completion is expected.

■ A daily formal review is conducted between the DM (team) and the planner (conducted in the morning regarding the previous day's route) to discuss what went well and not so well with the previous day's routes, the reasons why, and what resulting output (forward actions) are necessary to improve overall route completion.

■ Business targets regarding the number of drops per route and the percentage achievement of completed services for the depot are to be jointly owned by scheduling teams (NSM and STLs) and operations (RM and DMs), and at the individual depot level the DM and the planner, and where DM bonus structures apply, this anchor metric is included as bonus criteria to ensure full ownership (see also Chapter 8, "KPIs, the Balance Scorecard, and Basic Financial Models" and Chapter 12, "The Depot Manager Cadre").

■ A weekly formal review is to be conducted including either NSM/STL or both the RM/DM. This review will analyse route-scheduling performance trends for the previous week, previous rolling six weeks (drops per route per day scheduled, drops per route per day achieved percentage service level) with the aim to (a) compare results to depots of comparative size and geographical environment, (b) understand root causes to failures, and (c) agree on remedial actions and set targets for the next two weeks.

Which Organisational Model Is Best?

The centralised model provides better training, development, and team coverage and as this function is fundamental to any route-based logistics business and a critical lever to optimise profit generation and service excellence; ensuring a highly trained team of scheduling practitioners collectively adhering to best practice, the author recommends the central model having experienced both scenarios. However, the pragmatic answer is that in large businesses (ten-plus depots) whichever model is currently deployed, unless the existing team skill set and productivity (drops per route) are sub-optimal and in need of radial change, it is prudent to retain the existing model and focus on developing and improving processes and expertise rather than "uproot" an established methodology, and such change may take many months and prove costly and potentially negatively impact customer service throughout the transition period.

Planner Renumeration and Training

The pivotal importance of route scheduling and its impact on productivity and profitability is sometimes underestimated and subsequently insufficient attention is given to implementing the most appropriate organisational structure and leadership. Scheduler (planner) remuneration, if uncompetitive, is unlikely to attract or retain high calibre planners and attrition may be high as a result which will prove disruptive to service delivery, productivity, and generate seepage of key operational knowledge and skills. It is challenging to recruit established and experienced planners with readymade skills in scheduling theory and application, therefore developing a highly proficient team is best achieved with in-house formal training programs for both new and existing employees, supported by the software supplier and if necessary, by external logistics expertise. But having invested in training and upskilling schedulers, the business must implement tactics to retain this valuable cadre and avoid a brain drain.

To establish a robust training environment, senior management will need to consider the following.

- Engage with the routing software provider (ideally encompass this concept during contract negotiation to formalise the methodology and to achieve best cost) in order to design and deliver a training program so that planners learn all aspects of how best to use the software and ensure that with each future software upgrade, supplier training is refreshed appropriately.
- The Head of Scheduling together with the COO to design a training program and conduct detailed in-house training programs for newly recruited planners into the business supported by regular (at least twice yearly) training "boot-camps" for existing planners to ensure their understanding of software iterations, latest operational and scheduling team techniques. Importantly initiate planner performance metrics by depot, region, individual planner, and any subsets of planning teams. Incorporate a competitive environment with performance tables regarding productivity and output ratios and completed service percentage.
- The scheduling department is instrumental in driving operational performance improvement and therefore consider incentivisation schemes including a performance bonus rather than applying simple salary banding as this provides a genuine win-win for individual colleagues to enhance earnings and business via productivity improvement.
- It may be perceived as "unusual" or not company policy for non-managerial roles to receive bonuses, but it is worthy of consideration for this pivotal role. However, the scheme should be individual rather than "team" and must incorporate multiple metrics to ensure that any individual payment earned also benefits the business, consider therefore:
  1. Number of total drops (visits/jobs) scheduled (actual vs. target – daily and weekly).
  2. Actual number of total drops successfully completed (actual vs. target – daily and weekly).

3. Number of "second-attempt" drops completed within "X" time of first miss and percentage of second-attempt drops completed within SLA – weekly. This measure ensures that the planner does not focus simply on new incoming orders but is diligently "sweeping-up" failed first-time drops.
4. Number and percentage of total completed first attempt drops (actual vs. target – daily and weekly).
5. Include a team element (no more than 20%) that incorporates the service level for the depot for successfully achieved drops (actual vs. target – daily and weekly).

Consider how often the bonus pays out. This cadre is unlikely to be on high salaries, so the guideline is quarterly, so that the pay-out cycle is always "in-line-of-sight" and if the criteria is not achieved the next bonus potential is not too far away.

Manual vs. Software and Which Package?

Unless the numbers of vehicles per depot is less than ten and or the average time at each drop is c30 minutes plus (i.e., furniture delivery and installation), both parameters limit the number of drops per route (when loading, unloading, and break time is accounted for) that require scheduling; then introducing appropriate route scheduling software packages will increase productivity (number of average drops per vehicle route) where software has not been previously used, providing that the business follows a procurement process to select the most appropriate package to match the business service profile and, as is the case with telematics, the business does not pay too high a price for the package, ongoing licencing, and maintenance.

The author has deployed various software applications in various businesses that historically scheduled manually, achieving productivity improvements in the range of 10%–16%. It is important to understand accurately the baseline before introducing software solutions and establish target setting that measures success post implementation against the baseline, and that metrics are objective, and which can be evidenced. *Whilst savings in fuel and hours worked are obvious benefits, these variables may fluctuate for a variety of reasons other than solely scheduling; therefore, the primary focus and objective post implementation should be vehicle and route reduction leading to the physical removal of a vehicle(s) from the fleet. If a vehicle is removed, by definition the driver headcount will also be rationalised. If a depot has 20 vehicles before a software project is introduced in tandem with trained schedulers, genuine tangible benefit would be measured in the reduction of one or two vehicles (and commensurate heads). The removed fleet is "held" centrally, under fleet management auspices, to prevent continued use at the depot. The drops associated with original route(s) are absorbed across the remaining routes post a depot re-routing exercise with all residue routes completing more drops per route on average than before the exercise.*

Route scheduling software packages have been in existence for 20 plus years, and whilst they operate broadly in the same way, some are much better suited than others depending on the specific business application. They encompass algorithm "engines" that efficiently schedule high volumes of drops at a speed and at an accuracy that the human brain simply cannot replicate. Each logistics type business (that has a depot infrastructure and radial vehicle fleet) will have a unique set of operating variables that will influence the selection of the most suitable software package and, notwithstanding other decision factors such as price, aftersales care, training and system reliability, and up time, the operational variables that are core to determining the most suitable software solution include:

1. The number (volume) of drops per day/week that the package must process. If this number is in the tens of thousands, then some applications will simply not be designed to process such volume at requisite speed.

2. Whether the drop type is "bus-stop" like, which means entirely predictable and uniform each day and week, or whether the drops are ad-hoc or unpredictable and are therefore fluid on a daily basis and this landscape may be further complicated by changeable customer window times, multiple customer types, and varying services or product at varying customer locations. The less predictable the service environment, the more complex and sophisticated the routing solution will need to be.

3. The cut-off time between last customer order received "today" for delivery today, or more usually next day. Whilst some businesses may know their customer requirements several days or weeks in advance (much simpler to plan and for packages to schedule), other businesses may have an evening cut-off for next day's service or receive orders today for delivery the same day.

4. The number of "ad-hoc" customer requests that are received "today" (sometimes with a cut-off at noon) for delivery before close of business today (same day).
5. The number of operating variables that the supplier package may not be specifically designed to automatically deal with, and which may require either an operational procedural "workaround" or necessitate the supplier to create a bespoke upgrade (which will take time and add cost), examples might include, but limited to:
   1. Multiple vehicle models/types at a single depot each having defined operating rules and varying capacity limits regarding cargo,
   2. Multiple driver skill sets (specific licencing or certification enabling drive "A" only to operate vehicle type "B"),
   3. Varying load-related insurance limits on a per vehicle model basis,
   4. Customer restrictions (for example access vehicle height) limiting specific vehicle model entry to specific customer locations.

The variables outlined above illustrate the complexity involved in route scheduling and the importance therefore to best match the application to the current and potential future operational and customer service requirement.

The perfect-fit package is unlikely to be readily available unless the business has a predictable drop volume with a "bus-stop" type application; so an element of pragmatism is required to determine the "best-fit" package at the best price, and importantly, the suitability and compatibility of the supplier software package with existing business core IT systems, and whether these systems are managed/owned by a third party or company (in-house) owned and managed, and that they can interface to the software package. There is a myriad of suppliers in the marketplace, and it is important to conduct a full tender exercise including customer reference checking including visits to existing customer to personally witness the package "in action" and question other customers directly, and even when a preferred supplier status is achieved with one supplier, ensure to conduct a test pilot at one depot only before implementing more widely. Taking time to procure the right package and right supplier will pay dividends in the long term.

With so many route scheduling software providers in the market, it is recommended that the initial tender exercise be supported by the procurement and company IT teams and plan to conduct two to three rounds of selection and negotiation and be sure to fully understand the "aftersales" support capability, cost of package training, and willingness and capability to train, before making a final decision.

Do Not Blame the Scheduling Software, without First Examining Business Data Integrity

A prerequisite when preparing to introduce route-scheduling solutions is to ensure customer data integrity, the size and complexity of this task is usually underestimated, but without a robust data platform of current and accurate customer information, deploying a software solution prematurely will deliver sub-optimal results. The old adage of "rubbish in, rubbish out" has genuine pertinence; regrettably, businesses may be complacent in preparation, but you have been warned.

The following customer data tasks are necessary:

1. All terminated customer's data needs to be removed from the data set that will form part of the interface with the routing package.
2. All current customer data needs to be validated and accurate including:
   a. Address details
   b. Postcode
   c. Note: Some applications may require correct lat–long (latitude/longitude) coordinates.
   d. Contract service requirements, this may need separating into specific "field" subsets. What service, which products, frequency, etc.
   e. Window times. Important note – for best results, this data must not reflect necessarily what the depot team historically does, or what the staff anecdotally thinks the customer wants, but what contractually the customer has agreed, *providing the widest possible service window time is critical in order to optimise scheduling potential.*
   f. Special site instructions or access restrictions need to be current and accurate.
   g. Special driver training, driver skillset, licensing, or security clearance.
   h. Accurate time to conduct the on-site visit is crucial, if the system time incorporates "slack," it will restrict the number of drops per route the software will schedule.
3. On a regular basis (at least twice annually) post introduction, it is beneficial to revalidate (cleanse) the data set to ensure no erosion of data

integrity has taken place including the removal of data relevant to any customer locations lost since the last cleanse.

Scheduling Principles

Consider the following guidelines before implementing route scheduling software.

Proof of Concept

In businesses where route scheduling software is being introduced for the first time across multiple depots, ensure during contract negotiations with the supplier that the mobilisation is not "big-bang" but is predicated on a proof-of-concept pilot involving one (two depots maximum) depot to minimise business disruption and to ensure that the undoubted IT and operational teething issues are contained, fully resolved, and between business and supplier a jointly agreed methodology is formulated for future depot implementations. The pilot depot(s) can be promoted as a best-practice methodology, training hub that can support other teams. Improved scheduling results need to be achieved and sustained before moving out of a pilot phase and to ensure full depot management buy-in. The pilot will have more credibility if the depot is a large urban depot (the bigger the fleet, the better the potential saving) and the management team of the pilot depot must be an experienced, high-energy team that embrace change, they need to be involved early in the program, supportive of the concept, and eager to be at the vanguard of the change program.

The supplier will "promise" a potential improvement percentage during the sell phase, so it is important to establish an accurate baseline position for the pilot depot that both the business and the supplier endorse and mutually agree. If feasible, negotiate a monetary incentive if the promised percentage improvement above baseline is surpassed and monetary penalty, if it is not achieved within a specified timeframe. The guideline parameter for the baseline would be a duration of three months (the most recent three months is best, but avoid unusual volume months, for example peak trading, Christmas, Easter, etc.) and understand in detail any changes due to large contract wins or losses, the baseline needs to accurately reflect a normalised run rate but err, if any, on the upside, don't agree a "soft" baseline, formulate a realistic baseline that if improved will be genuine savings benefit. Agree the standard drops per route for the depot overall and the number of routes for each day of the week that represent the baseline. Gains are likely to be significant and achieved quickly post introduction with incremental improvement thereafter. The target for success must be measured in less routes and vehicles (and therefore less employees) on a same volume throughput basis, avoid measurement of savings in hours worked or miles saved, these are welcome but unlikely to be "dial-changing."

The Planner and Software Interface

No scheduling software package will produce optimum results without commitment from both supplier and business management teams to work really collaboratively during the planning and implementation phases, and in many business environments there are some variables that the software may not readily cope with, especially during the pilot phase as operational nuances are fully understood and need additional software changes from the supplier, remember it is a pilot for both supplier and business. Having an experienced planner during pilot to finesse routes and deal with nuanced issues is key to a successful implementation. The planners will need extensive training by the supplier on how to use the software, their knowledge needs to have genuine depth when the pilot commences, no software produces a perfect route, and the "first-cut" will always need manually finessing by the planner who will understand nuanced "real-life" elements that need consideration and which the software cannot take account of. However, the planner must be open-minded, the software will not be influenced by history or have a natural preference to route customer X on day Y because that's what the planner has always done; the software produces logical, efficient routes applying all the data that the business has "cleansed" and confirmed as good to go, resisting the urge to want to restrain the software, and create a route that resembles history is vital, the number one objective for the business in investing in the supplier's solution was to significantly improve the drops-per-route ratio and consequentially rationalise resources; if this is not achieved, there is zero point in investing, and whilst management must recognise the pivotal role of the planner in delivering success, management will need to educate the planner who must internalise the objective.

Driver Start Time

The software will calculate the most logical route to maximise the number of drops within the boundaries of the variables applied. Having flexibility with driver starting times rather than rigid and fixed start times is a positive benefit that will enhance productivity. Ideally it helps to provide the software a window of starting times (say within 1–2 hours) and which management can update drivers with once routing is completed and their start time is confirmed the day before go-live. If driver start times are fixed, it will inhibit optimum drops per driver day. However, if start times have to be fixed, then endeavour to have teams of drivers commencing, in staggered fashion, every 20 or 30 minutes (or at intervals that reflect the average time on depot to load) to provide a structured but flexible framework on which to schedule (see Chapter 4 – "Minimising Non-Productive Hours").

Setting SMVs[1] (Standard Minute Values) for Customer On-Site Time

There are three core elements to a route.

1. *Travel time* (stem mileage to and from the depot or home, and the radial mileage between drops). Scheduling packages have in the main perfected algorithms or link with road software packages (e.g. TomTom) to providing excellent road-mapping and travel-time capabilities incorporating multiple road speeds and reflecting peak-traffic flows. Usually, this element requires little intervention from business planners. Travel time is non-productive, it is a means to an end, the end being the customer location. The aim when route scheduling is to minimise non-productive time.

2. *In-depot and break time.* Including all depot time, loading, unloading and debrief, and break(s) time taken at the depot or during the route. The in-depot element is covered in detail in Chapter 4, "Minimising Non-Productive Time."

3. *Productive time.* The time at the customer site, this time is chargeable and revenue earning. The aim of scheduling is to maximise the number of occasions on site to optimise the revenue generated per route. The time on customer site can vary significantly depending on the service provided and it is critical that the time allocated in the software package is accurate and current, this is fundamental to achieving route optimisation. Every minute is important when scheduling routes. For

example, if the average number of customer visits per route is 20 and the system average time on site is eight minutes (160 minutes site time), but the actual time on site is seven minutes (140 minutes site time) the software is missing the opportunity (due to the business's inability to administer the data set accurately) of an addition of 1–2 drops (depending on inter-drop travel time) representing 5%–10% productivity loss, multiply this across all depot routes, and all depots and the waste is material. Every minute is genuinely pertinent.

It is important therefore to regularly review a proportion of actual drop times to determine a realistic average timing to input into the software package, and this process will require the engagement of depot management teams who will need to have a physical presence on-site with drivers, with stopwatch in hand, to time the activity whilst assessing driver ergonomics, parking habits, and walk times, to determine a realistic time on location. Ideally, the manager should actively participate and conduct sample services to verify the SMV (standard minute value) for each activity. If each depot manager and their team conduct an agreed sample number of on-site checks each quarter, the SMV data set can updated and maintained. Before the pilot commences, large enough sample of timings will be required to be conducted across all depot routes to ensure that on-location times are fair and realistic before commencement. This exercise may warrant support from colleagues from other depots and if necessary, a third party "time and motion" company (there are many on the market) to verify existing timings and ensure accuracy. The time on location is a pivotal variable, and ensuring its accuracy is fundamental to optimising results. Historic time on site, and or planner timings, are unlikely to be too tight or prohibitive, and likely, over the course of time, to have become loose and have slack. Therein lies a significant opportunity.

Two Methods of Deploying Scheduling Software

The first is fully integrated with core business systems and used daily with static planning practitioners. These are high-end packages requiring integration, they are used:

▪ Where the volume of daily drops is too large for human planners to produce efficient routes given the volume and or the complexity of variables. In this environment, it would be challenging for the business to cope efficiently in any circumstance without a scheduling system. The scheduling package is an integral and at the core of operations.

■ Where the routing package can cope effectively with business operational variables with an element of finessing by the planner(s). As a rule of thumb, a depot requires a minimum of ten or more operating vehicles with each route having on average ten or more drops of low predictability, the volume of daily drops requiring scheduling must be sufficiently large to justify the cost of installing the package, if the existing planning (manual) challenge is "light" and the planner is already producing efficient profitable routes, the cost of introducing a new routing methodology may not pay back. The larger the fleet, the greater the number and density of drops, and the more complex the variables, the greater the benefit is likely to be in introducing route-scheduling software.

The alternative method is to deploy software periodically (half yearly, or when significant volume fluctuations occur, for example a large contract win or loss). This package type is significantly less costly to procure, are effectively mobile, not static, and deployed via a roving experienced planning practitioner that visits depots with package in hand to a published timetable.

■ Where the complexity of operational variables renders daily routing too complex for software to produce meaningful route results quickly, or where cut-off time constraints are too tight to effectively use a high-end package.
■ Where route and or drop volume is not high enough to warrant the cost and capability of a high-end package, but where a software solution in tandem with an experienced practitioner can deliver productivity benefits.
■ Where volume and customer requirements are highly predictable and subject to little fluctuation or change. This enables a practitioner to visit periodically, re-set the route framework and which will remain stable enough for a local planner to manually route to a good standard until the practitioner returns.

Validating Route Efficiency

Scheduling packages usually incorporate easy-to-use post route analysis functionality to enable a comprehensive review of the planned versus actual route enabling planners to analyse route effectiveness and polish their finessing prowess. The examples in Figures 3.8 and 3.9 illustrate the type of data that good scheduling packages produce rapidly without fuss when combined effectively with telematics route feedback to provide a data set with which management can determine the root cause of missed drops and other route discrepancies with drivers during debrief.

Figure 3.8 illustrates an example final planned route. There are 22 drops programmed from a depot located in Cardiff and the data also indicates the software recommended time and location for the driver to take a break, and additionally the driver's home address is identified.

There were three missed drops on the route that day. If the reason for the missed services (see Figure 3.9) is due to inaccurate data, for example incorrect address or incorrect opening window times, the management can verify and correct to avoid future issues. However, missed services may also result from either driver error or deliberate avoidance, the rationale for which will require investigation at debrief and this route functionality is invaluable in determining the root cause.

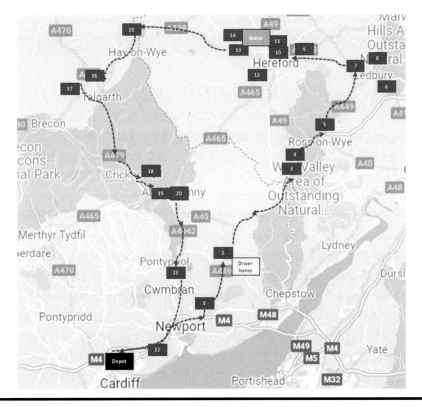

Figure 3.8   An example planned driver route with 20 drops from Cardiff depot.

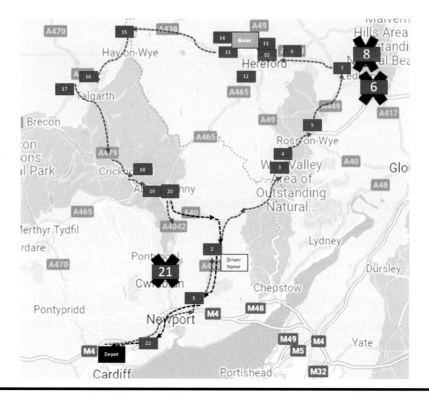

Figure 3.9   An example of the actual route sequence and missed drops planned in Figure 3.8.

In the example (Figure 3.9) there are three missed drops on the route, drop numbers 6, 8, and 21. Good practice would involve local depot management contacting customers 6 and 8 to verify customer opening times and, in this example, management did and both customers confirmed they were open for business that day and the opening hours were in line with the "system window" of 08.00–16.00; however, the driver entered a "reason-code" on the PDA entitled "customer closed." Analysis of telematics data indicated that the driver actually arrived at Ledbury at 07.30 and was questioned, at debrief, why he had not waited for thirty minutes until opening time. Drop 7 was open having a window of 07.00–17.00 which is why this particular drop was completed whilst drops 6 and 8 were reported as "closed."

Drop 21 was also missed with the driver entering a reason code "customer-closed." However, analysis revealed that Drop 21 was deliberately "missed" by driver. The driver had not taken the prescribed route and the telematics report indicated (refer to the black arrows) that he drove via the A449 not on the A402, and on investigation at debrief the reason given was

that "he was rushing to pick his child up from school" (his wife was alleg-
edly unwell and unable to collect the child from school) which coinciden-
tally is why he started his route 45 minutes earlier than the scheduled start
time and hence why arrived prematurely at Ledbury and decided not to wait
until 08.00 when both drops 6 and 8 would open. The driver failed to communicate his circumstances with management prior to starting the route, and
without the debrief process, supported by telematics and software functionality, the actual reason for the missed services would mostly likely not have
been discovered. In this example, the driver was appropriately disciplined
and future routes placed given a specific watching brief by the management
team. The add-value benefits of both software packages are powerful tools
enabling management to exert control by being data-led.

Every planned drop not completed requires investigation to determine
the root cause and ensure that appropriate remedial action is taken, this
action may be business fault, for example administrative oversight (incorrect
or inadequate customer details initially entered onto the system), driver fault
or customer fault (for example, a refused service, closed without warning,
or closed when the customer is planned to be open). In businesses where
this rigor has not been previously applied, the drilling down into each and
every miss may feel burdensome to management teams, but very quickly the
number of misses will reduce, and depot service performance improve. If
the customer data is accurate and current, and software and planner create
efficient but realistic routes, then unless there is a genuine incident beyond
the driver's control that is evidenced by management, the expectation must
be 100% route completion.

Every missed service may not result in a customer complaint; however,
a consecutive missed service for the same customer at the same location is highly likely to trigger a complaint and tarnish business reputation.
Therefore, every "missed" service is cause for concern and if the root cause
does not reside with customer, operational teams must take requisite remedial action to deal effectively and promptly to (a) rectify the miss and complete the service and (b) prevent a repeat. Every miss increases business
cost as at least two visits are required. Missed drops must be treated as high
priority and drivers must be aware and know that every miss will result in
an investigation (as in the example with Figure 3.9) at debrief, the messaging
must be overt and unrelenting.

When a missed service is "re-routed" for a second service, local management must ensure that the requisite driver is made aware of the importance
of this specific drop at start of the route and verify with the driver that

requisite product/parcel/consumable/equipment required to fulfil the service is onboard the vehicle.

"Miss" Notification

Good practice will ensure that the first time a missed service is escalated/ reported to local management is *not* during debrief when the driver returns to the depot. This is too late to effect any positive remedial action. A fundamental rule (that needs incorporating into the company handbook and or the operating manual, and rigorously applied by management) must be that the driver notifies the depot of *any* problem or reason which may result in a customer missed service, and this communication takes place whilst the driver is at the location and *before* he or she moves onto the subsequent drop. There can be zero tolerance for a "drive-by" without management knowledge and subsequent authorisation. This rule:

- Provides management the opportunity to contact the customer and resolve any entry issue before the driver departs and enables management to clarify if the customer is actually open or not. This action may squarely place fault with customer not service provider, and without the communication, process management would be unsighted.
- Provides support for the driver (especially useful for a trainee or driver attending a location for the first time) in finding a challenging address or facilitating access via customer contact if the customer information is incorrect for some reason.
- Enables management, not the driver, to determine the appropriate course of action to take, and,
- If the depot team agree that a "miss" is appropriate, the depot team can then facilitate an extra drop (if one is available but not previously on the planned route) to recover the drops-per-day target and maintain route productivity. This option may not be feasible in all businesses, but it can be a useful mechanism.

Depot Strategic Modelling

Many software packages incorporate sophisticated modelling tools that support strategic decision making. Functionality may include the capability to pinpoint optimum depot location when siting a new depot, calculating the optimum number of depots in relation to business volume and providing "before and after" routing scenarios when contemplating closing depots and rationalising the depot infrastructure.

There are several key factors that influence depot location and routing configuration:

1. Drop density, the number of services per square mile across the depot geography that require servicing each day/week, and the delivery/collection windows of customers.
2. The average number of miles per route and average miles and road type between services, and the duration in hours of the route including break and in-depot time in relation to driver contracted hours.
3. The average number of drops/services per route and aligned to this the average time at customer location.
4. The contractual length of the working day of drivers with consideration given to average OT hours, and home postcodes of existing drivers with a view on likely postcode areas of future drivers. Whether drivers work depot to depot, or home to depot, and understand if this arrangement is fixed or variable. For example, if home to depot, if the vehicle is not at capacity at the end of a route, can the driver be routed home to home for that day?
5. The opening hours of the depot, any operating hour constraints and average loading/unloading times.
6. Whether drivers have fixed start times or have flexible start times, and if the latter, is there a band that the start must fall into, for example 06.00–08.00. If start times are fixed, can they be staggered to optimise loading cycles, for example X drivers start at 06.00, and Y drivers start at 06.30, and so on.
7. The minimum or targeted service delivery (SLA) that the business is seeking to achieve, a 98% successful completion of services requires more certainty when routing, for example than a 90% target and this may, in-part, be linked with tightening the depot geographical boundary area.
8. Boundaries with neighbouring depots; how many neighbouring depots there are, and is there scope and appetite to adjust these boundaries, careful shuffling of outlying drops near the boundary can significantly improve a route(s) at one or more depots.
9. The profitability of the average route and consolidated profit of the depot; as the boundary and area square miles increase, and or the average miles per drop increases, the number of drops per route is likely to

decrease and with this profitability per route is diluted. This dilution is off set and may be more than compensated for, if boundary and drop changes result from rationalising a route(s) or closing a network depot and with it saving the associated overhead costs (e.g. management, rent, rates, utilities, depot ancillary staff, equipment), and these overhead savings exclude any benefit from reducing fleet and driver resource; however, the law of diminishing returns[2] will apply.

It is not possible to state what the optimum depot infrastructure is, each business will have varying service requirements regarding points 1–9 above; however, there are factors common to all businesses, the UK road network is fixed, increasing vehicle population and diminishing average travel times, population density is likely to impact most service businesses in a common way; therefore, it is logical to state that in order to sustain a high-throughput national service with stringent SLAs, it is unlikely that such a service can be successfully delivered and sustained with much less than the low twenties of depot locations. Figure 3.10 provides a strawman of what a basic national depot network might look like, incorporating smaller satellite locations (low-cost business units with single aperture loading shutter and small team) in rural areas.

The depot network (Figure 3.10) broadly mirrors the population density map illustrated in the bottom left-hand corner. Northern Ireland is serviceable with a single depot (the author has operated in NI previously with three companies) and Wales has a depot on the south coast near Cardiff to service the south and west coasts with a satellite near mid-Wales (in this example Shrewsbury) with Manchester servicing the North coast of Wales. The Highlands and Islands of Scotland are serviced in this model by local subcontractors (a methodology common to many businesses). North of Leeds, the road networks tend to run South-North rather than cross-country, hence the necessity for a satellite located at Carlisle.

In principle, the tighter the SLA, the greater the number of depots required, for example if services or products are required the same day, stem mileages will need to be lessened. From order placement, the product must be picked and or packed, loaded, and routes created post order cut-off, these activities all nibble away at time before the driver arrives at the depot and a wheel is turned to commence route. A long order to deliver lead-time provides more flexibility and more final-mile solutions.

If a business's infrastructure has depot numbers in the mid-high twenties, low thirties, or greater, there will, without question, be significant opportunity to rationalise the network, to close depots and save material

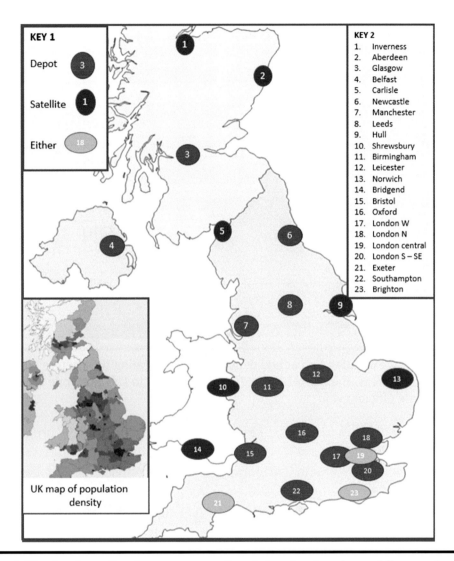

KEY 1

Depot	3
Satellite	1
Either	18

KEY 2

1. Inverness
2. Aberdeen
3. Glasgow
4. Belfast
5. Carlisle
6. Newcastle
7. Manchester
8. Leeds
9. Hull
10. Shrewsbury
11. Birmingham
12. Leicester
13. Norwich
14. Bridgend
15. Bristol
16. Oxford
17. London W
18. London N
19. London central
20. London S – SE
21. Exeter
22. Southampton
23. Brighton

UK map of population density

Figure 3.10   A schematic of a common national depot network providing service across the UK.

infrastructure costs with the residue network being leaner, more productive, and profitable through economy of scale. The author has overseen the successful closure of 40 plus UK depots across four businesses without detriment to service.

Rationalising the Depot Network

Most businesses, and all UK software scheduling programs, will route using the customer location address "postcode" and possibly the lat–long

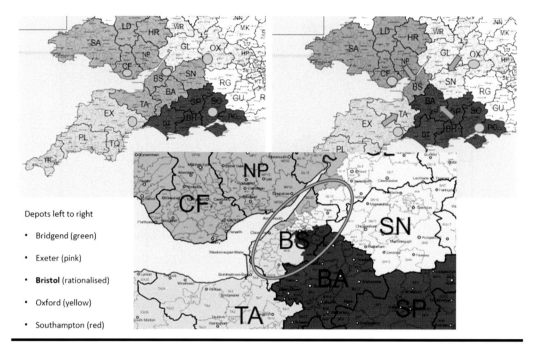

Depots left to right

• Bridgend (green)

• Exeter (pink)

• **Bristol** (rationalised)

• Oxford (yellow)

• Southampton (red)

Figure 3.11   An example of an actual depot closure indicating the "before and after" postcode depot areas, the Bristol city region was divided to sub-postcode area to optimise route efficiency.

coordinates as the key data feed. Postcode references in the UK are granular enough to pinpoint to street level and provides an excellent database.

Businesses using software programs are likely to divide depots geographically into service areas based on postcodes and sub-codes. To provide an example, the postcode maps in Figure 3.11 illustrate "rough-hand" the depot boundaries for five example depots (top-left caption). The illustration is a representation of an actual rationalisation project of a Bristol depot. The scheduling program enabled a modelling exercise to understand the post closure configuration, and to determine in advance, the optimum postcode boundary split post closure (top-right caption).

In practice, these programs enable strategic modelling to sub-code as the bottom picture illustrates with the BS (Bristol) codes sub-divided across four "sharing" depots.

The modelling exercise (referring to the example) enables the senior operations team to understand in detail the before and after routes per day and the potential savings to fleet comparatively between deploying either five and four depots, it will help calculate the total pre and post mileages and variations in average drop productivity per driver day. The author would expect such a modelling exercise to accurately predict the outcome within a sensitivity range of 3%–5%; therefore, once approved in principle, the project has a high degree of certainty.

When considering a potential depot rationalisation project, the following guideline principles need considering, and a financial business case will need to be constructed and presented to the company executive and or capex committee so that business leadership understand, in detail, the monetary benefit and ROI (return on investment), the timeline required to implement the change program, and the level of risk associated with the project. Companies may have strict ROI rules that govern such decisions, e.g. the project must pay back (generate profit beyond the cost of change) within a specific timeframe, and this requirement may be as challenging as 1–2 years, and if ROI timelines are tight, then such projects may be inextricably linked to the depot lease expiry date, so be cognisant of this early on during the concept phase and understand the lease end date, whilst exploring the potential to sub-lease the property.

Depot closure programs always contain an element of risk, but if thoroughly planned and sensitively executed with regard to colleague welfare and remuneration package, the operational and customer service risk should be manageable and low, but bottom-line improvement generally positive. Exec team members (especially if they have not experienced closure program previously) may be concerned about colleague moral and or employee disputes arising from associated redundancy programs, both concerns are legitimate and entirely understandable, and colleague welfare must be at the core of the project management's thinking; but if the rationale for a closure is logical, the communication with colleagues open and regular, and colleague renumeration packages are fair and equitable, colleagues in the main will cooperate positively. The 40 closure programs referenced previously were all executed on or ahead of time, within budget and delivered the expected ROI, and this was possible only with the buy-in and compliance of colleagues directly impacted by as a result of the program.

Some key pointers that will help minimise service disruption during the transition phases include:

1. Investigate depot lease expiry dates and whether a depot is leased or owned. If the latter, it may be sold to reap value, if the former, if the closure is implemented in line with lease expiry, then ongoing lease costs will be saved in full; however, if there is an extended lease period beyond the planned closure date, the ROI may be diluted and dependent on the likelihood to sub-let.

2. In broad terms, each depot closure should realise common savings including lease, rent, utility consumption, and ongoing premise R&M costs. Additionally, static colleagues including the local management team, administration and ancillary staff located on depot costs will be saved, but driver and fleet savings are likely to be negligible and dependent on geography and future route density.

3. Calculate redundancy costs associated with the closing depot and understand the company redundancy policy. With a depot closure, the static depot-based employees (management, administration, cleaners, and warehouse/stock roles) are likely to be considered for redundancy, but the situation with drivers is less straightforward as some drivers may present a case simply for depot transfer rather than redundancy depending on their home location vis-à-vis the nearest neighbouring depot, notwithstanding the possibility of alternative suitable employment in other parts of the business or associated group companies.

The 50-point guideline plan in Figure 3.12 is an example of what a basic pre-commencement concept plan might include for management teams to consider, support from a finance partner with cost calculations is helpful from the outset as good governance and give the CFO reassurance as to cost-calculation validity.

In Figure 3.12, the righthand column represents month one (P1 = period) of the project, in practice, these periods would extend for at least six months and until all task lines are completed. In the example only Phase 1 of five phases is input for illustrative purposes. It is not necessary to use a more sophisticated planning tool (e.g. Microsoft Project), sometimes simple is best, this plan needs reviewing by the project lead and all project participants with individual cells appropriately RAGGED to reflect progress. Tasks 1–50 reflect a starting position only, for a single depot closure, the number of tasks is likely to be in the range of 250–300 and as the project moves through the gritty implementation phases, some tasks will sub-divide to a more granular level, with new tasks emerging as the project unfolds.

Tasks not included in the example but need inclusion would be customer and internal company communications and union participative meetings and communication if the business has a union.

Notification to employees should take place as soon as is possible once the business has made a firm decision to approve a project, where a potential redundancy situation is involved, the business is obliged to communicate as soon as is practical and the trigger point for this is usually post executive

	Depot closure plan (for example purposes only)	Task owner	Phase	P1			
				wk1	wk2	wk3	wk4
1	**Business case & Exec approval**						
2	Complete business case with ROI (linked to task 32)	COO	3				
3	Include Project lead & key management participants	COO	3				
4	Present draft time-line & plan to Exec with ROI (linked with task 40)	COO	3				
5	Secure Exec tentative approval to proceed with planning phase (linked to task 17)	COO	3				
6	**Management structures post change**						
7	Agree pre & post provisional Depot management structures	Senior Ops team	2				
8	Determine which participants will form part of the implementation team & steering group	Senior Ops team	2				
9	Create NDA and have key participants sign before progressing.	HR	2				
10	Determine project team members (linked to task 24)	Senior Ops team	2				
11	**Communication & consultation**						
12	Agree consultation & redundancy criteria & process with HR	COO + HRD	4				
13	Assess potentail recruitment needs & time-line if leavers exceed expectation	Senior Ops team + HR	4				
14	Agree retention package (for whom, £ value of & qualifying criteria))	COO + HRD	4				
15	Create briefing packs & announcement paperwork with HR	HR	4				
16	Brief involved DMs & teams (ensure NDAs are pre-signed)	COO+RM with HR	4				
17	Announcement plan & rationale with time-line to potentially closure to all depot staff	COO	4				
18	Conduct consultation – 1 – driver & other roles potential transfer & redundancy	DM + local HR	4				
19	Consultation – round 2	DM + local HR	4				
20	Consultation – round 3	DM + local HR	4				
21	Confirm final decision with Exec / CEO regarding and update relevant colleagues of decision to – close or not to close	COO or RM + HR	4				
22	Plan repeat meetings (exclude consultations as appropriate) with receiving depots	Project lead	4				
23	**Project Management**						
24	Facilitate initial project meeting to on-board all critical team members	COO + HRD	3				
25	Set up weekly project meetings (2 phases – pre & post go-live) linked to tasks 5 & 17	Project lead (RM)	3				
26	Keep track of any exceptional cost items as they emerge	Financial "partner"	3				
27	**Scheduling & IT**						
28	Agree & set-up strategic modelling team	COO + RM + head of scheduling	1				
29	Commence modelling of pre / post closure depot and impact on neighbouring depots	Head of Scheduling (HoS)	1				
30	Complete modelling exercises & include financial results	HoS + finance partner	1				
31	Review with COO + RM to determine potential benefit or otherwise vs. risk	COO+RM+HoS+ finance partner	1				
32	Build business case & incorporate high-level route changes & timeline	HoS + finance partner	1				
33	Understand IT implications re data base & depot closure & post-code transfers	IT Director + HoS + COO + RM	1				
34	Model detailed route changes, route by route from closure depot to each receiving depot with time-line. They may require clusters of routes to optimise postcode density	HoS & team	3				
35	Review & update route changes as project commences & unfolds	HoS	3				
36	Produce weekly tracker, progress actual vs. plan and key requirements of other project participants at weekly meetings	HoS & team	3				
37	**Buidlings**						
38	Understand lease expiry & delapidations for traget closure depot	COO + Finance	1				
39	Estimate time-line to make-good "delaps" & costs, and whether a financial provision has been made	COO + Premises internal "owner"	1				
40	If lease expiry date exists, use as the deadline to achieve – it is a key milestone	COO + RM + finance partner	1				
41	Understand if any licences or certification requires "surrender" & process / timeline	RM	3				
42	Understand and create an IT timeline for removal / transfer comms & IT infrastructure	IT Director & team	3				
43	Create plan to run down stock / product in-line with plan	RM + DM	4				
44	Create a final removal & transfer plan of residue product / stock & equipment	RM + DM	4				
45	Understand and agree / cost + timeline alterations to receiving depots	RM + DMs	4				
46	Facilitate utility supplier & other equipment supplier visits to terminate / remove	RM + DMs	4				
47	Agree vehicle movement schedules in-line with route transfers & O licence changes	Head of Fleet	4				
48	**Go-live**						
49	Project plan to move from weekly measurement & reporting to daily	COO	5				
50	Commence project with first route transfer	All	5				

Figure 3.12   An example of a "starter" closure plan with generic elements for consideration.

(board decision) approval (in the example, this is Task 5), and this task is therefore linked to internal employee notification tasks, including the consultation process and a final business decision (Task 17 finalising at task 21).

Retention Payments

There are a few critical elements that ensure a smooth and successful closure program, one is meticulous overarching project planning in tandem with rigorous execution involving weekly mandatory meetings with all participants expected to keep pace and deliver on their individual compo-nent tasks, another is a detailed understanding of the "before and after" route configurations to accurately calculate how many, and which new routes are shifting to which depots, and by mapping employee home loca-tions who may qualify or be interested in transferring to a neighbouring depot, and finally, incorporating a fair retention package for each employee (irrespective of the length of service), working at the closure depot is key. Maintaining customer services throughout the program is paramount, cus-tomers should, in practice, barely notice the change if the plan is executed well, and to achieve this aim, the business must retain control of the employee leaver situation and avoid premature or wholesale colleague exodus.

The retention payment is a one-off benefit, paid in addition to notice periods and redundancy payments, and receipt is linked to a colleague remaining with the business until he or she is not required but in line with the communicated plan, this exit date may be at the end of the proj-ect (e.g. the exiting depot manager) or throughout the project phasing but in line with project requirements. The drivers located at the closing depot and who are not transferring to another depot and will leave are key to retain until inexperienced drivers in neighbouring depots are recruited and trained. Baked into the retention payment agreement is a provision includ-ing a reasonable notice period; it is not practical or fair simply to inform a driver that his or her services are no longer required, the author has usually adopted a four week notice period linked to an approximate phased time-line, which will be different for every driver and this process has worked with remarkable success. The retention payment value for a driver must be a sum sufficiently enticing so that the driver is willing to agree to the retention conditions and this sum will be fixed and not linked to the length of service so that employees with less than two year service are equally incentivised, longer serving employees enjoy bigger redundancy packages, and whilst this payment in total may be significant, it is small in comparison to the benefit derived from closing a depot and to ensure minimal service disruption.

Notes

1. The use of Time Standards. Roger Edgell. Managers-Net. Managers-net.com.
2. Samuelson, Paul A. 1994. The Classical Fallacy. *Journal of Economic Literature*, *32*, 620–639.

Chapter 4

Minimising Non-Productive Hours

Introduction

Every vehicle route in every route-based business comprises either productive time (drop time), when conducting the contracted service at the customer premises, or non-productive time, which is not directly chargeable and this latter element comprises:

1. Road travel time (including stem and radial mileage)
2. Depot time (start and or end of working day)
3. Return to depot mid-route
4. Driver break time(s)

The primary objective when scheduling and planning routes is to maximise productive time (chargeable) and minimise non-productive time. Through the application of Lean type processes to eradicate wasted time, non-productive in-depot time can be reduced with the saved time converted to increased available drop time which in turn may enable an extra drop(s) and thereby improve productivity. Increased productivity is a core objective for every depot management team, it is achieved either by delivering the same total drops with less resource (reducing fleet and commensurate employee numbers) or breathing extra drop capacity into depot operations (increased drops per hour ratio) without adding resource. Road travel (1) efficiencies are determined by the routing and scheduling team in conjunction with the

DOI: 10.4324/9781003323822-4

depot manager (DM), and guideline methodologies are discussed at length in Chapter 3, "Route Scheduling."

Whilst some business teams may view travel time as "productive" it implies a "fixed" element that cannot be subject to continual improvement and belies the fundamental aim of schedulers together with depot operational teams to constantly strive to find reductions in both the overall miles travelled and average miles per drop per route, thereby decreasing the average miles per drop ratio (an "anchor" key performance indicator (KPI) discussed in Chapter 8). *Every added drop per route increases route density and enhances route and depot profitability whilst reducing road travel time either in absolute or "miles per drop" ratio terms.* Road travel is not productive as it is not directly chargeable, but simply a means to an end, and management teams will more readily focus on continually reducing average miles per drop if they perceive it to be a non-productive cost element subject to continuous improvement.

Minimising On-Depot Time (Non-Productive Time)

Why Is This Important?

Because every non-productive minute "saved" (reduced) enables an additional productive minute at the customer premises, drop time. Whilst it is true that a proportion of each minute gained may be required to support extended travel time, in order to accommodate the additional drop(s), the largest portion of the saved minute is converted directly to increased productive time. Where drop density (i.e., urban areas) is naturally highest, the proportion of travel time used from every "saved minute" will be minimal or zero because the extra drop location will be at close proximity, and potentially on the same hight street.

In Figure 4.1, the time allocated to driver break, daily vehicle-check time, and the average customer "on-site" time remain constant. Focusing on reducing the key variable of "in-depot time" will automatically increase the available "drop time." The driver's total time at depot is described as "gate-to-gate" (GtG) time. This time commences when the driver first enters the depot gate until the driver and the vehicle leave the depot gate to either commence the route or travel home. At the start of the day, the gate-to-gate time encompasses various common driver tasks, including reporting for duty, retrieving equipment, checking the vehicle, visiting stores, loading,

Depot. X.	Monday		Route 1			
Note: All times measured in minutes, with shift-length fixed at eight (8) hours						
Route 1 Target time			Route 1 Baseline timings			Variance
Start of day GtG time	20	4%	*Start of day GtG time*	*30*	*6.5%*	10
Vehicle check time	8	2%	*Vehicle check time*	*8*	*2%*	0
Travel (drive time)	74	15%	*Travel (drive time)*	*68*	*14%*	-6
Drop time (at customer)	124	26%	*Drop time (at customer)*	*120*	*25%*	14
Break time	30	6%	*Break time*	*30*	*6%*	0
Travel (drive time)	96	20%	*Travel (drive time)*	*88*	*18%*	-8
Drop time	108	23%	*Drop time*	*102*	*21.5%*	6
End of shift GtG time	20	4%	*End of shift GtG time*	*34*	*7%*	14
Total time	**480**	**100%**	***Total time***	***480***	***100%***	**0**
Example route drops	39		*(Actual drops completed by route)*	*37*		4	5.4%
Average time on site	6			*6*		0	
Average drops per hour	4.9		*(no. of drops over all hours worked)*	*4.6*		0.3	6.5%
Total No. of Depot routes	42			*45*		3	6.7%

Figure 4.1   An example of depot route timings including target vs. actual Gate-to-Gate timings.

and driving out of the yard. Management teams have an appreciate of this cycle time and good practice will have the DM setting target GtG times for the driver and depot teams to achieve. The target time will differ by business and by depot and is dependent on several variables including the yard configuration and size, the type and complexity of the product required to load combined with average time to load, and the number of loading bays/docks in relation to the fleet number. In the example illustrated in Figure 4.1, the management target time per driver is 28 minutes (20 + 8) at the start of shift and 20 minutes at shift end, the variance of eight minutes is the allotted time to complete the mandatory vehicle safety check.

If a depot management team are uncertain about how to establish a realistic but challenging target GtG time, a simple in-depot "time-and-motion-study" (see Chapter 12) can be conducted by management in tandem with experienced drivers to record timings (using a stop watch and under normal conditions and not during peak season) for the various tasks that make up the GtG process, recording a variety of load types (if this scenario exists in-depot) to determine a realistic average time required to load. There are an abundance of easy-read explanations and studies which are easily accessible via the internet, and Lean and six-sigma are further discussed in Chapter 12. However, the task of recording actual GtG timings is simple and straightforward and can commence immediately (refer to Figure 4.4) without external or "specialist" support, this simple process requires a willingness by the DM to get a mini project started, initially participate in promoting the benefit and select trusted team members, and with the aid of a clip board and a basic Excel spreadsheet, a solid foundation can be achieved. Data collation covering a period of four full weeks is sufficient to provide a baseline position from which management can monitor ongoing trend improvement; it is not a prerequisite to conduct a full Lean exercise to generate a baseline position. Too few operational teams apply focus to optimising gate-to-gate times because the link between reducing time and increasing drop productivity is not readily made.

The important object is to determine a baseline, what the baseline GtG time is in itself not the end objective, but simply a starting position. This process is fundamentally one of the continual improvements from the baseline. The DM can target drivers and members of his or her team to improve in 10% "bitesize" incremental stages from the base position within a set period of say 4–6 weeks to achieve. If a national business with multiple depots, the initiative is best initiated at the regional or national level, but there is absolutely no barrier to a high-energy ambitious DM establishing a project unaided and from scratch. If promoted from senior leadership, why not nominate depot "champions" (a member of the depot management team) sponsored by the DM and thereafter set up agree metrics, measure progress, and publish depot results and acknowledge the most successful teams with suitable rewards for their success. The "reward" can be as straightforward recognition from senior management, a paid meal for the best depot team and their partners; whatever form the "thank-you" takes, it will help generate enthusiasm and a competitive edge between depots. DMs can share learning and methodologies as the project progresses with underperforming depots dragged onwards and gain momentum through adopting the good practice of their peers.

Each business type will have a unique customer on-site average time. A courier delivery business less than a minute, a hygiene services business circa six minutes (as an average within a broad range of 2–30), and a heating technician (boiler service) 30 minutes. In Figure 4.1, the average on-site time is set at six minutes and for the purpose of the example, remains constant. The gain of 24-four (24) minutes (consolidated start and end of day GtG improvement) per driver is achieved directly and solely by reducing GtG time, all of which is converted into two additional drops (6%); of the 24 minutes gained, 14 minutes (58%) is required for travel time to facilitate the extra two drops. However, even if just one additional drop is achieved per route through a GtG improvement exercise, this represents a significant business benefit worth securing. In Figure 4.1, there are 45 original routes on a Monday before the GtG time exercise is implemented, and one drop extra per route gained results in the depot requiring only 44 vehicles (a reduction of one) assuming volume throughput remains unchanged. A one route reduction reflects a minimum annual saving of c£40k for the depot. Multiply non-productive improvement across a depot network and the benefit can be material.

Start of Day GtG Time

For many businesses, this period of the day is pivotal in determining customer service; if the loading and despatch operation runs smoothly and quickly, the drivers will be in the best possible position to complete routes on time. Conversely, delays during start-of-day GtG time are unlikely to be fully regained on the road without increased OT costs, or with resulting missed services and customer complaints arising which will detract an already busy depot management team from their primary task of supporting drivers through the day in order to achieve the core objective of maximising route completion.

The driver tasks at start-of-day might include:

a. Clock in/sign in to formally commence work
b. Change into uniform (selected businesses)
c. Collecting equipment (trolley, PDA, vehicle keys/telematics fob, etc.)
d. Pre-brief (collect paperwork, receive special instructions)
e. Driver to complete defect report (if not completed as it should have been at end of day) if necessary and allocate and gather the replacement vehicle
f. Collect vehicle and conduct daily mandatory vehicle check if the vehicle is a non-starter change vehicle
g. Entering loading bay/loading area

h. Load customer product, deliveries, vehicle stock and consumables and exit loading bay/dock

i. Manoeuvre out of yard via the gate and start route

Depot operations vary in fleet size with the largest depots accommodating one hundred plus vehicles to load and or despatch at start of day ("start" in this context means shift-start time whether early morning, PM, or nightshift). There is a minimum of one driver for every vehicle (sometimes a "driver's mate"), plus warehouse activity with associated personnel and management team members, so depots are busy environments with lots of bustle, crowded restrooms, and multiple vehicular movements in the yard. In such an environment, it is easy for the less scrupulous driver to waste time finding little constructive to do; and if management are uncoordinated and not regimented and focused, many non-productive hours can be consumed during the despatch period. This lost time is easily given up and almost impossible to retrieve without adding unnecessarily to unplanned and expensive overtime costs to compensate at the back end of the shift. A late despatch operation may impact other depot activity such as warehouse good-in cycles or the next day's pick and pack operation causing significant cost and service implications.

Depots operate in daily repetitive cycles, and if one day's operation runs late, a domino effect can occur that may not be fully "caught-back" until the weekend and this will require unplanned costs. There is no reset button. Once a depot's daily equilibrium is disrupted, the collateral damage can spill into other days, so the key learning is to remain entirely focused on ensuring each day goes as close to plan as is possible. It is paramount therefore that the start-of-day operation is organised in a highly structured way and with management focus (including the depot manager's presence), with the objective to ensure minimum GtG time for each and every driver. There must be an activity plan for the despatch operation including specific driver start times and scheduled (target) in-loading bay times.

Assuming that vehicle loading is via a loading bay or loading dock, the despatch operation is defined by the number of docks (see Figure 4.2) versus the number of vehicles that must load via these docks. In Figure 4.2, there are 12 vehicles loading via four docks, and assuming only one vehicle can enter a loading bay at a time, three loading cycles or "waves" are required to complete the despatch operation.

The vehicle that is allocated to which "wave" is determined by the start time of each route (route-scheduling team). Driver start-times and the

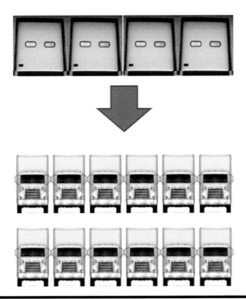

Figure 4.2   The depot loading cycle is defined by the fixed number of loading docks/ bays. The example ratio is 3:1 and therefore three loading cycles or "waves" are required. (Truck images: © Shutterstock.com. Used with Permission.)

loading sequence must not be a "free-for-all," the loading operation must be planned in advance and logical. Drivers arriving at depot long before their allocated start-time are to be discouraged and when they do, they need to wait in the restroom until their "wave" is ready to load and only when directed by the yard marshal; otherwise, drivers will quickly appreciate that the despatch process is not robust, and they, not the management team, determine the loading sequence.

Drivers start-times need to be staggered in line with the number of loading waves to avoid paying colleagues to sit in the restroom; however, management might consider a plus-one scenario per wave (in Figure 4.2, five drivers start each wave not four), with the earliest scheduled route determining which driver from the subsequent wave is to be included; this plus-one ploy provides continuity of loading in the event of an unexpected absence or a late starter. If all allocated drivers do arrive on time, the plus-one "spare" driver might productively assist with the despatch process, for example start manoeuvring the next wave vehicles into a pre-dock entry position with engine running to save time and identify a potential non-starter. It is important that as one wave exits the docks the next wave is ready to enter with drivers already in-cab, and in winter, with engines running, if drivers of the next wave are wandering aimlessly in-yard or looking for or starting vehicles then valuable time is wasted and the GtG target may be missed.

Alternatively, if the plus-one concept is not implemented, a management team member (or appointed warehouse stand-in) ensures that the driverless vehicle is loaded to schedule by personally driving the vehicle into dock to load, and thereby ready to depart when the driver arrives, with the driver's lateness addressed by management during debrief (Chapter 8). The caveat with this process is that in the event of a subsequent issue with missing product supposedly loaded identifying root cause and culprit is rendered more complicated.

A route-scheduling program is logic based and will produce (in tandem with a planning practitioner) the most coherent and optimal routing schedule which must be adhered to and not subject to "on-the-day" changes at the whim of a driver or despatch manager. Adhere to the plan, deviations increase non-productive time. If the despatch plan requires finessing, agree to this as a management team post-despatch and initiate the new process going forward but avoid on-the-day "tweaking" unless it is to resolve unavoidable incidences, for example vehicle breaksdowns, loading bay damage and or breakdown, etc.

Calculate the average GtG time including the time to load, by way of example assume 30 minutes relating to Figure 4.1 and plan the operation to run in 30-minute cycles with matching driver start-times.

- If the driver for route 1 is scheduled to leave depot at c06.00 to commence route,
- The driver's start time is 05.30. The start of day GtG time is targeted at 28 minutes including a vehicle check of 8 minutes, a 05.30 start provides a two-minute grace period.

If the operation provides scope to pre-load vehicles so that drivers can collect their vehicles and leave depot immediately, this minimises GtG time. The author has managed some large depots deploying a skeleton evening/night shift operation with part of their duties including the fuelling and pre-loading of every vehicle and parking them in a "first-out" of the yard sequence so that driver GtG time is minimal. The additional benefit is that non-starting vehicles are discovered in good time and replacements substituted before the despatch operation commences. To implement this model, the day's routes need planning and finessing with adequate time (this is dependent on the time at which the last customer orders are received) to enable the pick and pack operation to run concurrently. Where drivers do not load their own vehicle, the loading methodology must be meticulous and "failsafe" (incorporating a secondary check, and ideally protected with CCTV) to prevent customer missed services or missed products and or unscrupulous drivers claiming product was not loaded with resulting "shrinkage."

Give consideration for the parking layout within the depot yard. Allocate vehicles to defined bays if feasible and spend a little money to line-marking dedicated vehicle spaces and ensure vehicles are parked sequentially with earliest departures nearest loading bays (or if pre-loaded nearest to depot gates), this eradicates the "excuse" for colleagues having to search for keys and or shuffle vehicles around the yard rather than getting the right vehicle in the allocated dock and to plan.

As a rule, vehicles should be fuelled at shift end not at shift start (if fuelling is yard-based), it will become another pinch point if the depot has a bunker, and a fuelling que may further inhibit yard mobility and restrict the despatch operation; at shift end colleagues are keener to complete tasks and focused on getting home.

Figure 4.3 illustrates a basic three-point communication management "triangle" with tactical deployment of management, and or allocated support staff, to aid a smooth despatch GtG process.

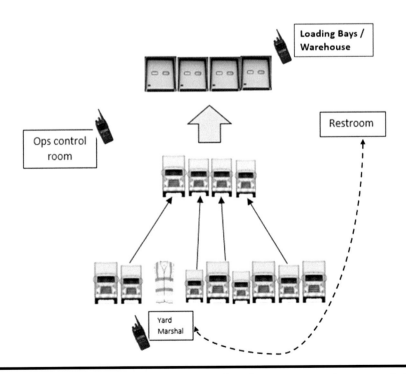

Figure 4.3   An example of the management triangle to oversee the start-of-day despatch operation. (Truck images: © Shutterstock.com. Used with Permission.)

Radios are useful in this application as they enable constant "hands-free" listening across the three key points of control. The proximity of the three points may not be in direct line of sight so the radio is a great asset. The configuration and size of every warehouse, loading bay, and yard combination is unique as is the presence (or otherwise) and the location of changing rooms and canteens/restrooms, so the number of managers (or supporting team members) required in each depot to coordinate operations will vary. In the example above, the yard "Marshal" role is responsible also for monitoring and controlling the restroom due to the distance and the relatively low driver numbers. Other suggested "holders" of a radio that help facilitate a smooth GtG execution might include the DM and the fleet maintenance technician (if one is deployed) or sub-contractor that is on depot to provide rapid response to mechanical issues, especially during the winter when "cold-starts" can be problematic.

A depot start-of-day GtG process of clearing the depot may take anything from 30 minutes (single wave) to 2–3 hours depending on the number of vehicles despatched via the number of available docks. During this despatch period, depot teams need to focus on as few other ancillary tasks that distract from despatch duties, or that otherwise can be completed later in the day. For example, goods-in receipts, non-essential training activity, audits (internal or external), and any depot visitors or suppliers should be avoided.

Having the depot manager actively involved during despatch is conducive to success, a depot manager arriving for work post-despatch of the fleet is not demonstrating a positive example to others and certainly not "leading from the front." The sublime messaging from the DM's absence is that this process is not critical. Whilst the depot manager does not need to be one of the radio-triangle team, neither should he or she be locked away in an office oblivious to problems. Providing a presence on site (across yard, warehouse, and restroom) with radio in hand and listening in, ready to engage with and motivate colleagues, and resolve immediate queries and disputes is invaluable and will aid pace and momentum. Avoid the need for a colleague to go to the DM office to resolve a query pay or a leave request (this may waste 10–20 minutes of a colleague's time and tie up the DM or the member of management and defer route departure time). However, do capture any query "on the move" and importantly take a note with a promise to respond the same day, and critically make sure the query is responded to and the promise kept via a call whilst on route or during driver debrief.

New starters and trainees require relatively more encouragement throughout their training period and having the DM present is both gratifying and motivational for colleagues, another important by-product from the DM's presence is that he/she will learn what actually takes place during this critical time of the day rather than listening to anecdotes; and this learning will enable the DM to implement, shape, and actively participate in ongoing improvements and changes to the GtG process in collaboration with colleagues.

The three radio communication points most commonly deployed are:

▪ *Control Room.* This area may have various titles and shared functions, but most depots have an area where the planning and management team reside, route documentation is retained, and driver debrief occurs. Only one manager should be required during start of day and associated tasks may include:
  – Exchange of equipment (PDA, vehicle keys, telematics fob)
  – Clock-on/clock-off manual or machine/process
  – The day's route/journey documentation (if not electronic directly via PDA) issued
  – Special instructions for a driver on a specific route
  – Change of vehicle notification and vehicle key issue
  – Receiving absence notifications and taking responsibility to replace or determine what to do with the route
  – Facilitate any vehicle exchanges due to non-start, etc.
  The manager in the control room is likely to be the most senior of the three points of the triangle.

▪ *Goods-out (loading docks/bays).* This may be linked to the main warehouse, or an internal dry area designated to loading, both are likely to incorporate a "Stores" with customer product and driver/installer consumables. The area may "double" as goods-in at various times during the day. Whether loading docks, loading bays, or a designated area of the external yard, the loading function is likely to be operated by non-driving dedicated staff.

Most vehicle loading is likely to be via loading bays or docks and neither loading operation is visible from the yard or control room. The loading element will consume the majority of the despatch GtG time and is therefore a critical element and which needs a specific target time for driver and warehouse colleagues to achieve. In the example, 30 minutes (28) GtG time, the in-bay loading element is likely to be 12–15 minutes (circa 50% of GtG time), and any delays in-bay directly impact the route and will have a negative domino effect on every other vehicle planned to use the same loading bay. The loading manager (or appointee) has the important responsibility to ensure no delays when in-bay and that vehicle loads are ready and checked in good time to meet the schedule, and this manager must be responsible to achieve the specific in-loading bay target time for all vehicles being despatched.

▪ *Yard Marshall.* This role may be permanent (with the colleague conducting other duties once the GtG process is complete), or part time.

GtG Metrics

Measuring GtG time daily, by wave (cycle) and individual drivers, is necessary to understand the root cause of specific "pinch points" and why more general delays occur, and additionally to generate a dataset suitable for management to gauge the success or otherwise of the day's activity, a simple metric is required with actual timings compared to planned timings, see Figure 4.4. In this example, each wave has four vehicles, and each vehicle/driver is allotted a specific bay (numbered one to four). Only the first two loading waves are illustrated in Figure 4.4.

The four points of measurement are:

▪ Start-time (clock-on time). Arrival at depot, or the point which signifies start of shift and the point from which the driver is being paid, this commences the GtG cycle.

▪ The time of arrival at the control room (this location may not differ from the start-time point depending on the depot configuration) and where route-related documents and or PDA are collected, and specific customer instructions relayed. If delays occur at this point,

Running	Bay No.	Driver	Start P	Start A	Variance	C room P	C room A	Variance	Loading P	Loading A	Variance	In bay P	In Bay A	Depart P	Depart A	Variance	GtG Plan	GtG Act	
A	1	x	5.30	5.30	0	5.30	5.30	0	5.40	5.38	2	20	20	6.00	5.59	1	30	29	1
B	2	xx	5.30	5.30	0	5.30	5.30	0	5.40	5.39	1	20	21	6.00	6.00	0	30	30	0
C	3	xxx	5.30	5.30	0	5.30	5.20	0	5.40	5.40	0	20	23	6.00	6.04	(4)	30	34	(4)
D	4	xxxx	5.30	5.35	(5)	5.30	5.35	(5)	5.40	5.43	(3)	20	17	6.00	6.00	0	30	30	0
E	1	y	6.00	6.00	0	6.00	6.00	0	6.10	6.10	0	20	18	6.30	6.29	1	30	29	1
F	2	yy	6.00	6.10	(10)	6.00	6.10	(10)	6.10	6.13	(10)	20	24	6.30	6.37	(7)	30	37	(7)
G	3	yyy	6.00	6.00	0	6.00	6.00	0	6.10	6.09	0	20	21	6.30	6.30	0	30	30	0
H	4	yyyy	6.00	5.57	0	6.00	5.57	0	6.10	6.12	0	20	27	6.30	6.40	(10)	30	40	(10)
Totaal variance in minutes					(15)			(15)			(4)		(11)			(19)			(19)
Average variance					(2)			(2)		Average loading time		21.4				Average GtG time			32.4

Figure 4.4 An example of a start-of-day GtG planned vs. actual schedule. Where P equals planned time and A equals actual time.

the manager in the control room will record. Ideally driver start-time would be triggered at the control room and in the presence of a manager.

■ Entry time to loading bay (in Figure 4.4, it is titled "Loading P"). The yard marshal will record this time and it is helpful if the "capture sheet" includes space to incorporate a one-line explanation regarding late running, for example the previous vehicle (registration) delayed loading, or driver X arrived late, or vehicle defect, etc. This will aid the management team's review of the despatch operation.

■ Time in the loading bay. This is always the longest segment of time within the despatch process and requires its own sub-target, in the example in Figure 4.4, this target time is 20 minutes.

■ Exit the depot gate. When the vehicle and driver leave the depot gate to commence their route and close the GtG cycle, theoretically this time should be within a minute or two of the loading bay exit time as there should be no remaining tasks to complete and nothing preventing immediate exit from depot, but nonetheless the timing point is worth recording for clarification.

Whilst the overall average GtG time in the example is 32 minutes (bottom righthand cell) per driver against a target of 30 minutes (7%) and at first glance the variance appears to be reasonable overall; however, the benefit of timing segmentation enables management to pinpoint specific root cause. The area of concern is that five out of eight (63%) drivers exceed the target of 20 minutes in-bay time with the highest negative variance being driver "yyyy" who exceed target by seven minutes (35%). Whether the root cause is warehouse, driver or process related, or a combination of factors, without data capture, it is challenging for management to understand the root cause and determine how best to improve. Trending these metrics over time will indicate whether the depot team is improving the GtG process from a base position where the depot's performance stands comparatively to other depots.

The end of day/shift GtG process is a reverse sequence of the start of day with some different tasks (driver debrief), but nonetheless, it is important to measure in similar fashion; the sequence upon re-entering the depot gate might encompass,

a. Enter depot and refuel if a bunker facility exists (if bunker is busy skip and try post unloading)

b. Entering the loading bay/loading area
c. Unload the collected product/re-stock product and consumables
d. Conduct vehicle defect sheet if necessary
e. *Attend driver debrief desk, at end of debrief conduct mini pre-brief for next day's route*
f. Return equipment if assigned (trolley, PDA, vehicle keys/telematics fob) at start of day
g. Change of uniform
h. Clock-off (end duty) – It is helpful if this task can be incorporated at the end of the debrief process to provide an agreed end of duty time and pay point.

A frequent problem experienced at many depots at the end of day is excessive queuing at pinch points when the number of vehicles returning in an hour exceed the number of available loading bays. Whether routes are manually or software scheduled, the estimated return time is known in advance and management can therefore plot the expected return phasing to understand, in advance, the impact and plan resourcing at depot to best manage these peaks, Figure 4.5 provides an example assuming 32 routes are planned on the day.

In Figure 4.5, the hours between 13.00 and 15.00 indicate a minimal risk of waiting time if routes broadly maintain plan; however, the next two hours (16.00–18.00) may benefit from the presence of a yard marshall working in conjunction with the warehouse team to minimise waiting time. Management must actively participate in managing these peaks rather than hope that the 20 drivers, expected to return in a two-hour window, will efficiently manage themselves. Each day of the week will have a unique routing profile and route numbers and the return-to-depot profile is likely to vary significantly, so this profile requires mapping for each day as illustrated in Figure 4.6.

Returning routes require the same diligence with regard metrics to measure depot returning GtG performance. Figure 4.7 illustrates the first eight vehicles upon their return to depot.

Time of day (per hour)	13.00	14.00	15.00	16.00	17.00	18.00	19.00
No. of vehicles returning to depot each hour.	1	2	5	9	11	3	1

Figure 4.5   An example of a day's expected vehicle return-to-depot sequence.

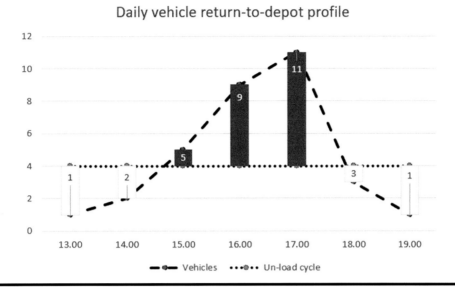

Figure 4.6 Daily vehicle return-to-depot profile.

Running	Bay No.	Driver	Return to depot Plan	Return to depot Act	Variance	Bay entry time	In-Bay P	In-Bay A	Variance	Debrief start time	Debrief	Planned Hours	Paid Hrs	Variance	GtG Plan	GtG Act	
A	1	x	13.30	13.20	10	13.21	20	22	(2)	13.45	8	8.30	8.25	5	30	30	0
B	2	xx	14.00	14.10	(10)	14.12	20	20	0	14.35	10	9.00	9.15	(15)	30	35	(5)
C	3	xxx	14.45	14.40	5	14.40	20	20	0	15.05	8	9.45	9.45	0	30	33	(3)
D	4	xx xx	15.00	15.15	(15)	15.22	20	32	(12)	16.00	16	9.50	10.40	(50)	30	61	(31)
E	1	Y	15.10	15.10	0	15.03	20	20	0	15.25	7	9.30	9.30	0	30	22	8
F	2	Yy	15.35	15.50	(15)	15.55	20	22	(2)	16.20	10	9.55	10.20	(25)	30	40	(10)
G	3	yyy	15.45	15.35	10	15.36	20	20	0	16.00	8	10.15	10.10	5	30	33	(3)
H	1	yy	15.52	15.50	2	15.51	20	23	(3)	16.16	12	10.22	10.30	(8)	30	38	(8)
		Total variance in minutes			(13)			177			Total minutes paid beyond plan				(80)	**Ave GtG**	**36.5**	
			Average		(2)			22										

Figure 4.7 An example of end of day GtG actual timings vs. planned.

The assumptions used in Figure 4.7 are that

■ When calculating paid hours, any driver starting before the scheduled start-time is paid only from the scheduled start time, arriving early is a personal decision and is unpaid. The route is created logically via scheduling software, and driver start-time is determined by the estimated travel time from the depot to the first drop plus the target GtG time, there is zero advantage to customers or the business in starting before the allotted time, it will simply result in waiting time at customer premises. E.g., in Figure 4.4 (start of day), the driver aligned with running order "h" starts early at 05.57 but the scheduled start time is 06.00 which is when pay commences.

■ Figure 4.7 assumes that any requisite vehicle re-stocking and equipment return is completed before debrief commences and therefore close of debrief marks the end of the working day and when pay ends. Encompassing end of day at debrief means that a manager corroborates "finish time" and subsequently driver pay will be accurate, and useful statistical analysis can be completed regarding the day's worked and paid hours almost immediately post close of day.

■ Minor rounding is applied in minutes regarding finish time. This process is common is many businesses, and renders pay calculation and administration more straightforward to process.

Ensuring a formal and robust process to verify worked vs. paid hours is fundamental. This gap analysis provides an opportunity to save cost by ensuring that "under-worked hours" (paid but not worked) is as close to zero as is feasible. Incorporating the sign-off task as an integral part of the debrief process also helps sustain the debrief process as a mandatory function, where local management may not entirely buy-in to the process. Measuring hours paid against plan (actual hours vs. the budgeted hours) is an anchor KPI (also see Chapter 8 and Chapter 12).

There is a direct link between minimising non-productive time and achieving planned/budgeted costs. At the depot level, there are limited "dial-changing" opportunities, gains are generally achieved through incremental improvement, meticulous attention to detail, and a gritty determination of the local team to grind out success from the daily operational routine.

In Figure 4.7 which illustrates "eight driver results" (representing 25% of the 32 drivers at depot) for one specific day, the data indicates a negative net variance to paid hours of 80 minutes (1.3 hours) against plan. At first glance, it may appear benign but extrapolate this trend across the depot (32 not eight drivers) and it equates to 5.2 hours for the day and assuming a low average cost per hour plus on-cost (NI and pension) of 12 pounds (£12.00), the single day reflects a negative impact of £62.40; extrapolated over 260 days (average working days per year) and this modest variance increases to £16,224 without including any associated overhead costs for fleet and fuel. In some businesses this cost would equal 80% of the annual cost of an employee, but if the business has 20 depots each with an average of 32 drivers and all perform equally, the annual impact is a staggering £324,480.

Monitoring and controlling the in-depot GtG process will deliver small incremental improvements that will over time generate a local positive cost and productivity impact in any route-based business.

Further analysis of Figure 4.7 suggests that the root cause of the overall poor GtG process is connected to just two of the eight drivers. Driver "xxxx" (running order "d") started the route five minutes late (Figure 4.4), and during the day, this lateness is compounded with the return to depot 15 minutes later than schedule. The driver's unload time in-bay was 60% over plan at 32 minutes, and debrief is subsequently (but understandably) extended in duration as management must investigate in detail the reasons for the driver's seemingly mediocre performance. The example does not focus on drop data (number of planned drops) or the driver's success rate (number of missed drops) against plan but if several misses had occurred then this driver really has had an "off-day." Regrettably the mediocre performance comes at a cost, repeated delays result in this driver being the highest paid in number of hours whilst producing the worse negative variance in paid-to-planned hours. Additionally, the delays in-yard and bay (end of day GtG) have a knock-on impact to driver "yyyy" (running order "h") who is unable to enter the planned bay (Bay 4) but is required to be reallocated to Bay 1 (Figure 4.7).

These eight drivers reviewed in Figure 4.7 reflect the early part of the return cycle when depot activity is the lightest (Figures 4.5 and 4.6), the following two hours represent peak yard and in-bay activity, so the delay caused by one driver has a potential negative domino impact on returning drivers later in the schedule and compounded additional OT hours. In depots with inadequate yard space and or limited bays (neither scenario is uncommon), an unstructured, unmanaged return-to-depot process can, in a worse-case scenario, cause queuing of vehicles in the road adjacent to the depot entrance resulting in unwarranted overtime payments and frustrated drivers wanting to go home.

To summarise, the in-depot gate-to-gate time and process at both start and end of day reflect core operational activity in virtually any depot environment and is an activity that needs active managing in a structured way. Allowing the process to "self-manage" will increase costs, reduce productivity, and may disenfranchise driving colleagues. Any reduction in non-productive time will directly increase available productive (customer site time) time and help increase the drops per route ratio and with it depot profitability.

Avoid Returning to Depot to Take a Break

The practice of returning to depot mid-route to take a break has become less common as businesses operate more efficiently, but if the business you

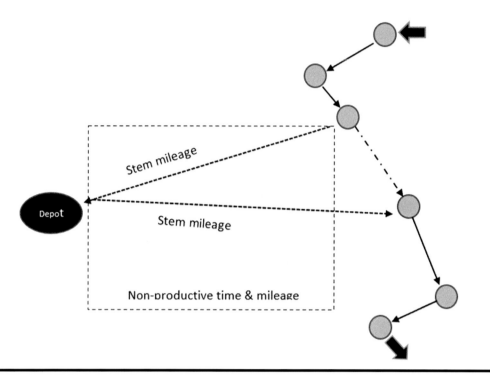

Figure 4.8   Avoid returning to depot mid-route to eliminate wasted stem mileage.

are working at still accepts this practice, then work towards its elimination unless there is a compelling justification not to do so. Figure 4.8 illustrates why this practice compounds non-productive time.

Returning to depot to take a break will result in less drops being planned. Not only are there two additional stem journeys that erode potential productive time, but there is likely to be an element of wasted time on depot beyond the planned activity, 5–10 minutes, beyond the official break time or used talking to other colleagues, can elapse with relative ease and combined with the non-productive stem journey time, the percentage of the day wasted can be material. Endeavour therefore to enforce breaks within the scheduled route, and across a range of time, for example a two-hour window approximately at the route's mid-point, to provide planners some flexibility (so if the shift is eight hours in duration schedule a break within the range of hours 3–5) and if toilet facilities are a requirement, explore the use of customer sites or retail carparks or fast-food locations with free car parking. In practice, experienced drivers with knowledge of a route quickly appreciate the various "watering-holes" along the route.

Chapter 5

Driver Debrief

Introduction

Whilst a brief chapter nonetheless the topic of Driver Debrief warrants a dedicated chapter in recognition of the pivotal function this process provides. All non-driving depot colleagues work statically at depot, within defined physical boundaries and have structured management support which is close to hand. Management and non-driving employees interact regularly and often break times are shared events and taken on the premises.

Conversely drivers are not a "captive cadre" and many relish working in an "unsupervised" environment and like not being confined to a fixed location; therefore, without a structured and robust communication process, drivers will perform their duties in a loosely controlled environment with little meaningful management/colleague interaction. Whilst "on the road," it is possible to communicate of course via phone or PDA, but for a quality, personal interaction, there is no substitute for a face-to-face dialogue and there are only two opportunities to do this during a working day, either at the start or end of the working shift, and if drivers start their route from home with their LCV, their opportunity is limited to end of day.

At start of day, the priority for depot management is to ensure that drivers commence their respective routes on time and with as few interruptions or delays as is feasible, and which may prevent leaving depot to schedule and thereby impact the success or otherwise of completing their route without missing a service. See Chapter 4, "Minimising Non-productive Time." Start of day needs to operate as close to a production environment as possible in order to get drivers in and out of loading docks to plan out of depot, it is not a time to dwell and discuss issues that are not related specifically with the day's route. Every depot manager will know that if you get the drivers to commence their respective route on time you are giving all depot colleagues the best chance of a trouble-free day and your customers the best chance of on time service.

Driver debrief is a formal interactive process between a driver and a member of the depot management team conducted daily after route completion and during which the driver's performance for the day is reviewed, customer location issues or customer requests recorded, and matters of wellbeing discussed, e.g. holiday requests or other personal matters. It is feasible to conduct a debrief session over the phone (if drivers work home-to-home for example, or as a tactic to encourage zero misses) but at least one debrief each week needs to be a face-to-face interaction, and all trainee drivers or drivers with subpar performance and or failing to achieve full drop completion (a route with any missed service) need to attend depot with the debrief conducted by a manager, not administrator.

Figure 5.1 is an example of a typical debrief form; this document template may be either a hard copy (paper based) or completed via a PDA or

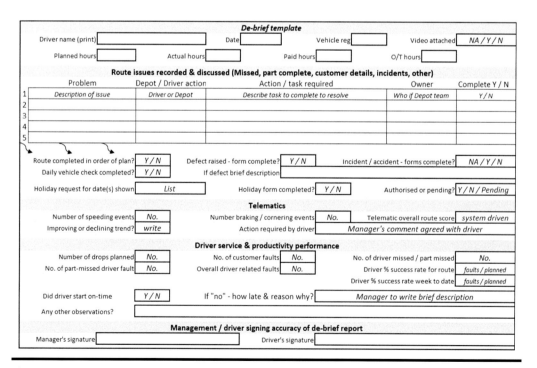

Figure 5.1   Example of a generic driver debrief template.

computer screen whilst at the depot. The example is generic and in practice each business will tailor the document to reflect the unique characteristics of the business.

Essential Output from the Debrief Process

The essential data capture during this formal end-of-day interface must include:

1. Missed or part complete drops/services and the reason for. Note, each miss should have been notified to depot management whilst the driver was at the customer location and before they depart for the next drop; if the driver has not notified the depot, this reflects a misdemeanour (if it does not in your business review the employee handbook and or employee contract and seek to change) and requires specific discussion at debrief. The benefit of notification whilst at location is that the depot team may be able to call the customer assist in getting driver access or as a minimum to confirm if the premises are closed or open; alternatively, the team can provide address or directions via the customer if the driver is struggling to find the exact address location. If after following the above process management agree (whilst driver is at the location) the drop will be "missed," the management team may be able to allocate an additional substitute customer drop (not previously on the route) to maintain route productivity; not all businesses will be able to achieve this aim, but if it is feasible, the option should be explored. This latter process will also help deter non-genuine "missed" requests if the driver appreciates that a potential outcome is to be awarded an alternative job to complete.

2. Location/address and or "window" time inaccuracies need identifying and the correct information immediately correcting on the customer address database to prevent a repeated failure. This feedback from drivers is key in maintaining an accurate database, and it is positive if management act upon this feedback and update the database within 24 working hours if it is not practical to do so in "real time." This will prevent a repeated failure, demonstrate a positive benefit of debrief, encourage further feedback from the driver, and enhance management's credibility. Every issue identified at debrief requiring management which is not resolved in real time must be recorded on a depot

De-brief task monitor							
Date	Vehicle reg or route no.	Driver name	Manager name	Issue & resolution	Target completion date	By whom	Outstanding or completed
				Description & action required		Driver name or manager's name	Blank or date completed

Figure 5.2   Example of management debrief "task monitor" data capture document.

debrief "task monitor" so that management can ensure that all tasks are meticulously recorded, and the depot manager is able to verify that the agreed corrective action has been completed. The data capture sheet is straightforward, and an example is provided in Figure 5.2.

3. All product/stock and consumable shortages that contributed to a service being part and not fully completed of a service needs rerouting asap once the missing product, etc. is verified as being at the depot, or management need to order. The customer needs informing (if they are not aware), and management need to understand the root cause as to why the product/stock, etc. was not onboard the vehicle at start of route.

4. Ensure that all basic driver working-day tasks and associated documentation have been completed and documentation accurate, these include:
   a. The daily vehicle check,
   b. The vehicle defect form (if required),
   c. The incident/accident form (if required),
   d. Drop related documentation (where a PDA is not in use and a paper trail is required).

5. That any relevant driver "life-admin" has been efficiently dealt with and recorded, for example holiday leave requests, new or replacement PPE.

6. Telematics route feedback including driver scores and incidents of harsh breaking, cornering, acceleration, and all speeding incidences discussed.

7. Driver overall service and productivity performance for the day and whether the trend is improving or worsening.

8. Driver start-time vs. planned start-time, and overall route scheduled time vs. actual hours worked, with a rounded discussion where variance is significant.

9. Return of equipment and PDA with validation that all are in good working order.

10. Close out the driver's working day and agree driver shift completion time.

Other Debrief Related Benefits

The debrief process provides the opportunity to be much more than simply an administrative exercise, it is *the* interface with a remote colleague where management can demonstrate leadership, promote new working processes and procedures, and take a genuine interest in and care for a colleague:

1. Making sure management take the time to say, "thank you" for a job "well done" when the driver produces a "clean-sheet" with no missed drops or has had a strong overall performance or excellent telematics score with zero speeding events, or the depot team have received positive customer feedback regarding his or her attitude or performance.
2. Enquire or seek update about a driver's general well-being or previously known situation or illness and check on the driver's family or home situation; if the driver is facing challenges "at home," it is likely to be reflected in work performance so an appreciation of this and requisite understanding is not only the right thing to do as one human to another, but genuine concern from management will be recognised, appreciated, and reciprocated.
3. Drivers in training and or induction will benefit from this touch point. People have different learning speeds, and some drivers will take longer than others to reach full output during their induction programme, and some may require secondary training and support, and the debrief interface provides a mechanism to establish driver needs and helps build confidence, and if possible, the depot manager (DM) should personally conduct a debrief with each trainee at least once each week throughout induction until the DM is satisfied as to the colleague's progress and comfort level.

How Long Should Debrief Take?

On average 8–10 minutes; however, the debrief does need to take as long as is required in order to deal with issues arising and specific driver needs; however, in large depots, there can be many debriefs to conduct and during the peak period (1–3 hours) of drivers returning to depot, there may be a pinch point of drivers vs. managers, so to help "process" quickly and to encourage good driver performance (zero missed drops), conduct zero missed performance via a phone-in debrief, unless there is a specific request from the driver to meet management, remembering of course to say thank you for a job well done.

Drivers that have had a mediocre performance and or traffic incidents/accidents, speeding events, or received a public/customer complaint on the day do need to expect a physical debrief, and management should wish to investigate such matters thoroughly, and more complicated debrief sessions may warrant 15–20 minutes, and occasionally may morph into a pre-disciplinary process.

Who Should Conduct the Debrief?

It is important that depot management do not allocate the debrief task to administrators but take ownership of this key interface in order to demonstrate both the importance of the process, and importantly reaffirm their genuine interest in their driving colleagues' performance and well-being. This task should be one management want to do rather than feel obliged to do, or to find reasons to abdicate responsibility for.

In most depots (and therefore most route-based businesses), drivers represent the majority of the workforce; it is inconceivable therefore that management would assume it wise or prudent to allow what is a mostly remote workforce that interfaces directly with customers on the front-line to work unsupervised and with scant communication, and to expect anything other than a sub-optimal depot performance.

In businesses that have not implemented driver debrief previously, some depot managers may raise the objection that they "don't have time," but debrief is a fundamental and essential process and once bedded into the operating culture and daily operating rhythm of depot life, it will enhance driver productivity, driver morale, driver absence, reduce attrition rates, and provide the principle mechanism for management to promote and reinforce company values, quality standards, and core operating procedures.

HGV Tachograph Analysis

The days when managers examined tachographs (tachos) is granular detail personally by hand have largely been replaced with the advent of a myriad of suppliers that perform this service remotely and produce a raft of useful key performance indicators (KPIs) and reports including lists of infringements by driver by category to enable management to provide driver feedback and take any action necessary.

However, the law for HGVs regarding driving and rest hours and tachograph use[1] is fundamental and a legal requirement and therefore management must ensure that the Tacho is accurately signed and dated, rest periods duly taken, and that driving time is not exceeding the permitted hours, and these basic checks should be completed upon the driver's return to depot irrespective of the need to collate tachos and ensure that every day has been properly accounted for by the driver before issuing them to the supplier for further inspection. The company and O-licence holder has a duty and responsibility to enforce adherence to driving and rest hours' regulations.

There are many publications regarding driver hours and tachograph analysis, so this book is deliberately scant on embellishing these matters, needless to say that where HGV drivers work at depot, the debrief process is equally meaningful and basic Tachograph administration and supply analysis feedback will be incorporated into the debrief process.

Note

1. https://www.gov.uk/drivers-hours, https://www.gov.uk/GB domestic rules GOV.UK. https://www.gov.uk/drivers/hours/en-rules.

Chapter 6

Customer Service

Introduction

> The single most important thing to remember about any enterprise is that results exist only on the outside. The result of the business is a satisfied customer. The result of a hospital is a healed patient. Inside an enterprise there are only costs.[1]

Drucker's words bring into focus the fundamental point that a business exists because of its customers and the "reason for being" is the service provided for the customer. Without the customer there is no business. In a route-based depot business, the reason for being is the service and or product being installed, delivered to, or collected from the customer, or customer's customer location. The business depot infrastructure, its fleet of vehicles, drivers, technicians, a myriad of third-party suppliers together with a whole host of supporting internal departmental functions collaborate in a complex web-like network to provide a means to an end, to service the customer.

Whether you work in the haulage, third-party logistics (3PL), or one of a myriad of service sector businesses operating with a depot infrastructure (i.e., hygiene, security, CIT, telecommunication, etc.), delivering service excellence consistently is fundamental to retaining existing customers and winning new customer contracts. TNT used to proport, via a strapline on their vehicles, that "our only product is service," and whether your company is simply delivering and or collecting product as parcel businesses do, the essence encapsulated in this slogan is pertinent to any route-based business. Customers want the right product or service, delivered consistently in full and on time, every time, and performed by a competent, trained individual

DOI: 10.4324/9781003323822-6

equipped with appropriate PPE and tools in a professional and courteous manner.

If products form part of the service (whether manufactured in-house or via a third-party), the quality and reliability of the product is fundamental, and the functionality must exactly match specification; additionally, customers demand and deserve their suppliers achieve the basic contractual service level agreements (SLAs) including:

■ On-time delivery or collection, this means arriving on the right day and within the contracted window-time, with right product, and with a competent driver.
■ Trained staff fully equipped and competent to provide a professional on-site service that meets the contractual specification, with the person suitably qualified and meeting all security and quality requirements.
■ Services to be completed in full consistently.
■ In the event that s service issue does arise, the supplier is honest and straightforward in communicating the failure as soon as is practical, whilst initiating a prompt recovery that fulfils the service obligation, and capable enough to address the root cause and prevent repeat failures.
■ That service statistics and customer key performance indicator (KPI) reporting is accurate, uncomplicated, and published consistently, on time, and in line with the contract.

Customers will quickly complain if service(s) are late or incomplete or if the driver's attitude and attire is not professional, and customers are justified in doing so. Customers pay an agreed price for the service and contracts will often include strict SLAs and indeed many customers will enforce penalty clauses for late, missed, or part-complete services.

Customer revenue funds employee salaries and management bonuses and colleagues may need reminding of this fact on occasion, the customer is not the enemy and has every right to complain if service is not meeting the SLA. Businesses operating from a depot infrastructure rarely exist in a monopoly environment therefore the customer usually has a choice of suppliers and can take their service to a competitor at contract end, or during contract if a breach-of-contract clause permits should service fall consistently below SLA without rectification.

Logistics companies, or services sector businesses, should avoid a scenario where they are competing for new contracts based predominantly on price; reducing pricing or competing at lower-quartile pricing devalues the market for all players and may, ultimately, negatively impact the businesses' ability for future investment in equipment and innovation. Lowering prices usually means lowering costs, and eventually, this may inhibit operational teams from delivering the expected service performance.

Wider economic forces continue to drive fuel prices upwards, and the advent of alternative fuel derived vehicles will raise costs, and in recent times, it has become more common for governments drive the minimum wage ever upwards, and these factors nibble away at business profitability. Striving to be "best-in-class" is one strategy for a business to differentiate itself from the competing pack, offer a unique selling proposition (USP[2]) is another, and some businesses may have a unique or innovative product (functionality or installation) that helps sustain pricing; but being perceived by customers as an "also-ran" from a core service perspective is no longer a viable proposition in the service sector. Providing poor service at low cost is rarely a sustainable proposition. To be recognised as delivering the "best" service in the market, a business must be able to evidence service excellence through robust KPI reporting whilst being utterly and consistently reliable.

Harry Selfridge's principle that the customer is always right[3] resonates today; the customer's perception of the service delivered by the supplier will directly influence their decision making and attitude at contract renewal. As a minimum requirement, service must meet SLA consistently and providing timely and accurate, easy-to-read KPIs that evidence the service provision is key to formulating the customer's perception (Figure 6.1).

Sales colleagues will be energised and confident if they genuinely believe that their operational colleagues can and do deliver to the agreed SLAs consistently, nothing deflates a salesperson more than having to spend time during a customer visit defending poor operational service (sub-SLA) as this creates an environment focused on negativity and which inhibits discussion regarding new opportunities for organic growth, it simply nibbles away at eroding the business's credibility and customer's trust.

That said, no business can afford or indeed should provide excellent or "best-in-class" service at any cost, this directly impacts profitability through inefficiency. Any operations management team can deliver good service at any cost; but service providers, and specifically operations management teams, must strive to achieve both core objectives, to deliver service at or better than contracted SLA and at "optimum cost," evidenced through efficiency ratios (refer to Chapter 8). The phrase "lowest-cost operator" is sometimes expounded but the two phrases reflect different metrics, the ratio method will take the size, complexity, and geographical footprint of

Category	The KPI	Commentary	RAG Drumbeat	RAG week, period & YTD	RAG DM Bonus
Service	% of scheduled drops completed	Target 99%. To be measured at individual driver level, per depot, region and nationally each working day, with summary weekly, period and YTD performance.	✓	✓	
Service*	% of daily contracted / required drops completed	Target 96-98%. The business TBC. The internal target should be greater % than is contracted with customers. To be measured at depot, region and nationally each working day, with summary weekly, period and YTD performance. An anchor KPI usually shared with major customers by customer, and across all customers as a company national average.	✓	✓	✓
Service*	Drops per driver day	Target TBC by business but linked directly with scheduling teams. This target will differ by depot depending on route density and average miles between drops. Measured by driver, depot, region and nationally. Increase target incrementally over time.	✓	✓	
Service*	Drops per hour worked	Target TBC by business but linked directly to scheduling. This target will differ by depot depending on route density and average miles between drops. Measured by driver, depot, region and nationally.	✓	✓	
Service	No. of first time drops not completed that are >3 days late	Each day "scheduled" to include today's contracted and "catch-up" drops from previous day(s) plus ad-hoc and special requests. It is important as a "check-KPI" that any contracted first-time drops missed are identified by schedulers and recovered next day.	✓	✓	
Service*	No. of drops contracted but not routed	The target must be zero. All contracted drops must be scheduled daily and with a realistic probability of being completed, but this is an important check-KPI to warn senior management of an early "red-flag".	✓	✓	
Service	No. of complaints raised	A basic KPI with the target number TBC by the business but will be related to depot drops, Fleet number and complexity of services.	✓	✓	
Service	Ratio of complaints raised against Depot over completed drops	The anchor Complaint KPI. Target TBC by business but a guideline target is complaint numbers to trend @ sub 0.05% of total completed drops.	✓	✓	✓
Service	Number of complaints issued to Depot not resolved in 3+ days	Target zero. This "check KPI" provides a red-flag to senior management if Depot teams are failing to keep pace with inbound customer failures	✓		

Figure 6.1   Guideline service and complaint KPIs with reporting frequency. Note: There are seven recommended KPIs to apply to the depot manager (DM) bonus scheme if such schemes operate, see Chapter 12.

the business, and customer mix and product range into consideration; the lowest-cost operator aspiration is one-dimensional. The basic premise of this book is to provide guideline methodologies that help operational business teams deliver great service efficiently.

Chapter 7 ("Managing Complaints") illustrates a process to help manage operational customer complaints, a facet inextricably linked to the customer's perception of "providing great service" and Chapter 8 includes a guideline suite for service KPIs, one subset of which is complaint KPIs illustrated in Chapter 7, Figure 7.1.

Notes

1. Drucker, Peter F. 2001. *The Essential Drucker.* New York: Harper Business.
2. Levitt, Theodore. 1986. *The Marketing Imagination.* New York: Free Press. "Reinventing your personal brand." March 2011. Harvard Business review.
3. Craven, Robert. 2002. *Customer Is King: How to Exceed Their Expectations.* London: Virgin Book.

Managing Complaints

Introduction

Businesses may have existing internal metrics that monitor the level of service they deliver but there is no better measure than receiving direct feedback from the customer giving their view on the service they receive, the feedback may not always be palatable, but there should be no hiding place when it comes to complaints, and if a business is going to retain and grow customers, it must learn to listen to feedback constructively and positively address the root cause. A business that is selling "service" needs genuine customer critique to provide management a window through which they can clearly see how their performance is judged from those who are "looking in" from the outside. An example of a comprehensive customer engagement philosophy was created by Reichheld[1] applying the concept of NPS (Net Promoter Score). To extract maximum benefit from NPS, the concept requires full engagement from every business department and function including Operations. There are many publications that examine NPS and competing feedback, and there is no need therefore to regurgitate them in this book.

The author has worked in several businesses deploying NPS and is an advocate, but for operations management to extract the maximum benefit from its introduction, additional layers of analysis are needed within the operations function in order to extract maximum benefit and be able to drill down to the source of a complaint in order to achieve lasting resolution. This chapter will provide a practical mechanism to help understand the root cause of a complaint, and by trending resolution results, operational management are able to evaluate complaint data and implement business wide

DOI: 10.4324/9781003323822-7

solutions to prevent similar future service failures. This process does not replace NPS; it is a necessary overlayer for operational teams to help them extract full value from NPS and to best resolve negative customer feedback; and this simple methodology can also be implemented independently if the business that does not have a formal complaints mechanism.

Inbound (customer feedback) complaints are usually channelled through the business call centre or contact centre (sometimes referred to as the "customer service centre" or the service department) which is the repository of the majority of inbound complaints, and in larger businesses that may warrant a dedicated complaints team, this team is likely to be a subset of customer services.

Figure 7.1 illustrates the generic flow of data that commonly bridges the customer service and operational teams regarding complaint management,

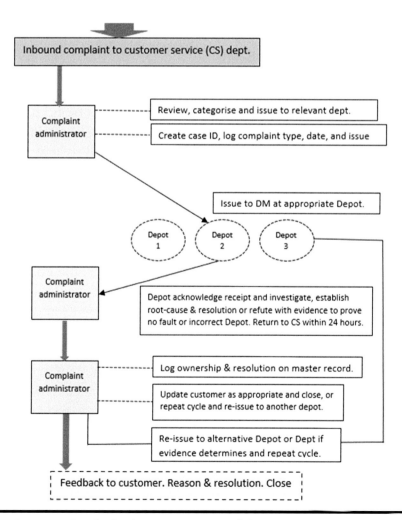

Figure 7.1   An example of a basic customer complaint process.

each complaint received will usually be issued with a "case number" or unique identification reference that will enable the specific "case" to be tracked until resolution.

Complaints reflect a perceived or genuine failure with a process, a person, or an IT system, and a complaint may pinpoint a failing in any business areas, for example:

- The Finance dept. (credit or payment queries, invoicing errors, or queries),
- The Customer Service (CS) dept. (speed of answering calls or mails, CS operative attitude or communication failure, an error during order receipt or subsequent processing thereof, failure of a CS operative to respond in a timely manner),
- The Sales and Marketing dept. (sales team member slow to quote or misquoting, failing to communicate as promised, or salesperson attitude),
- Product related; if products are integral to the service, insufficient stock to satisfy order, product quality, breakdown, wrong product, or model delivered, or reliability of post installation, or inferior quality or late installation.

The Operations department will have the majority of colleagues, the most "moving-parts," and will receive the majority of complaints, and whilst these may be specific to the business environment, the 22 complaint types illustrated in Figure 7.2 are likely to reflect the most common operational complaint types.

Every customer complaint reflects a process or people failing and warrants urgent review, a complaint is a seed of dissatisfaction which if repeated or not resolved quickly and efficiently may germinate within the customer and tarnish the business's reputation. Customer employees interact in the same way that colleagues in your business communicate, it takes just one dissatisfied person at a customer to generate wider negativity, and within a short space of time many people within the customer organisation will hear this dissatisfaction and once a supplier's reputation is tarnished it is challenging to regain a customer's confidence. All businesses experience service failings on occasion and customers in the main are sage enough to understand this fact, but being seen to be a responsive supplier, attentive and resolving failures quickly and professionally, including addressing the root cause, is likely to turn a negative incident into a positive view of the business and its people; therefore, treating every complaint with positivity and genuine

Operations	Complaint categorisation	Complaint source Customer or member of public (MoP)
Driver related	Poor driving	Customer or MoP
	Poor parking	Customer or MoP
	Driver attitude / behaviour	Customer or MoP
	Lack of or absence of PPE	Customer
	Not adhering to customer site rules	Customer
	Not suitably trained to conduct tasks	Customer
	Not suitably qualified, accredited or licenced to perform task, attend site	Customer
	Inadequate, broken or wrong equipment	Customer
	Not completing customer paperwork	Customer
	Not adhering to Covid rules (site or business)	Customer or MoP
	Incorrect product / stock delivered	Customer
Service Related	Missed or late service	Customer
	Repeated missed service	Customer
	Incomplete or part service (product, location or failure to carry-out all elements of the service)	Customer
	Poor quality service on site	Customer
	Wrong time and or wrong day	Customer
Service specific	Promised special service missed or late	Customer
	Urgent or second response service failed	Customer
	Special instructions not adhered to	Customer
Vehicle and / or driver	Cleanliness or condition of vehicle	Customer or MOP
	Vehicle has had an incident / accident whilst on premises (with object or another vehicle)	Customer or MOP
	Incorrect vehicle / access issues	Customer

Figure 7.2   Common operational complaints.

urgency it not simply the right thing to do, and no more than the customer deserves, but this rapid response will deliver tangible and positive benefit.

Internal rectification of a complaint may warrant additional personnel training and or process changes to prevent reoccurrence, but this reflects the evolutionary process that good businesses follow through continual improvement.[2] In large multi-depot operations providing tens of thousands of drops/ services each month, complaints are likely to trickle continually into the business and resolving these rapidly but resolutely will require a strong service ethic from all colleagues working across operational teams.

Each business will design a complaints process to reflect its particular requirements, but as a guideline, the following elements are recommended.

1. Every complaint is formally recorded and registered to a complaint "master" record before being issued with a unique and sequential ID number in order to track progress through to resolution. Receipt of the complaint must include data capturing the date and time received, and name of the colleague receiving and recording the complaint. This task is completed on the day of receipt (Day 1), it will be recorded, examined, and issued to the appropriate department, and if the Operations department, issued to the appropriate depot.

2. By close of Day 2, the receiving depot will acknowledge receipt and verify that the complaint is pertinent to the depot, and if not, respond quickly to the issuer in order that it might be forwarded to the correct depot team. The receiving depot team will investigate content, accept, or refute responsibility, and within 24 hours (excluding weekends or bank holidays) of receipt, provide in writing to the issuer a root cause, resolution, and what remedial action (internal to the business) is to be taken, by whom and when.

   The depot manager (DM) will coordinate with issuer to agree if the CS dept. or the depot communicate with customer regarding the root cause and rectification, to ensure that coherent feedback and resolution is executed asap.

   Internal action may include a change of process, interviewing of depot employees, re-ordering of equipment or stock, and result in a disciplinary matter, but this detail is to be fully documented with details of the driving colleague, vehicle registration recorded so that trends of individual performance and or behaviour can be maintained and monitored. The 80/20 rule is likely to apply if the complaint origin is colleague based, with a relatively small number of colleagues being responsible for a disproportionate number of customer related failings, and in order to eradicate these trends, it is essential to measure the root cause to the granularity of individual colleague.

3. On Day 3 the complaint administrator will provide formal feedback to the customer (unless the investigation has been re-routed and in which case, the administrator will provide a progress update and notify that the formal response date will be Day 5).

By Day 5 (excluding weekends) the complaint should be fully resolved from the customer's perspective however, internal learning points will be collated and discussed each week at one of the daily drumbeat calls, and each month a formal operations meeting will be convened (see Figure 7.3) in

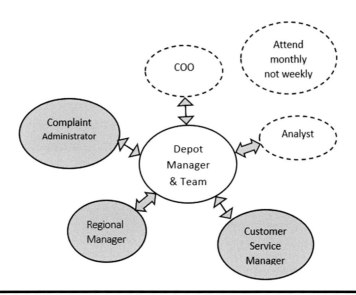

Figure 7.3   Monthly complaints meeting attendees.

similar fashion to the periodic fleet call to assess complaint trends and performance by depot.

When measuring complaint performance on a depot-by-depot basis, it is useful to review the number of complaints, but as depots have varying numbers of fleet and volume density, the most balanced measure of depot performance is via a ratio of actual complaint numbers over the total number of completed and part-completed (do not use the higher planned figures) drops/services, Figure 7.4 provides an example.

The example in Figure 7.4 indicates that depot 2 has the highest number of complaints in period 2, depot 1 has significantly more drivers and completed services than depots 2 and 3, but the complaints ratio (driver working days over completed services in the period) for depot 2 accumulatively at the end of P2 is the lowest of the three depots at 0.043%. As a guideline, the initial target for a depot team to aim for is sub <0.05% ratio percentage goal. Once achieved, the targets can be tweaked periodically to incrementally improve performance.

The summary depot data provides a good overall view of depot performance, but more detailed analysis is required to discover the root cause at the individual depot level, and only with this level of granularity will management teams have the requisite data to sustain improvement. The categorisation in Figure 7.2 illustrates the variety of failure types at the depot level, but the single most pertinent classification is to monitor depot complaints at the individual driver, as shown in Figure 7.5.

Depots	Period 1				Period 2				YTD		
	No. Drops	No. of drivers	No. of complaints	% complaints / drops	No. Drops	No. of drivers	No. of complaints	% complaints / drops	No. drops	No. of complaints	% complaints / drops
Depot 1	9,200	20	5	0.054%	9,350	20	7	0.075%	18,550	12	0.065%
Depot 2	18,700	40	9	0.048%	18,600	40	7	0.038%	37,300	16	0.043%
Depot 3	15,100	32	5	0.033%	15,250	32	9	0.059%	30,350	14	0.046%
Totals	43,000	92	19	0.044%	43,200	92	23	0.053%	86,200	42	0.049%

Figure 7.4   An example of complaint measure at the depot level applying a ratio of complaints/services.

Depot 1	Period 1			Period 2			YTD		
	No. Drops	No. of complaints	% complaints / drops	No. Drops	No. of complaints	% complaints / drops	No. drops	No. of complaints	% complaints / drops
Driver A	460	1	0.217%	420	0	0.000%	880	1	0.114%
Driver B	480	0	0.000%	454	0	0.000%	934	0	0.000%
Driver C	410	0	0.000%	416	0	0.000%	826	0	0.000%
Totals	1,350	1	0.074%	1,290	0	0.000%	2,640	1	0.038%
All depot 1 driver totals	9,200	5	0.054%	9,350	7	0.075%	18,550	12	0.065%

Figure 7.5   An example of complaint analysis at a single depot and to an individual driver.

The majority of drivers at each depot will have, in all probability, zero complaints recorded against them, and this process will quickly identify drivers that are repeat "offenders." There are 20 drivers at depot 1 (Figure 7.4), so the sample of three drivers in Figure 7.5 is sufficient as an example; two drivers are complaint "free," and driver A has one of the five complaints relating to depot 1 in period 1 producing a 0.217% ratio. A single driver may become a source of multiple complaints if competence and or behaviour is poor, but by drilling down to the individual driver, trends will quickly emerge which would otherwise be problematic to identify and certainly not at speed.

Notes

1. Reichheld, Fred. 2006. *The Ultimate Question*, and Reichheld, Fred, and Markey, Rob. 2011. *The Ultimate Question 2.0 – How Net Promoter Companies Thrive in a Customer Driven World*. Bain & Company.
2. Juran, Joseph M. 1974. *Quality Control Handbook*. New York: McGraw Hill. OCLC. 6th Edition. 2010. Imai Masaaki. 1977. *Gemba Kaizen: A Commonsense, Low-Cost Approach to Management*. New York: McGraw Hill.

Chapter 8

KPIs, the Balance Scorecard, and Basic Financial Models

Introduction

W. Edwards Deming wrote (*The New Economics*) that "it is wrong to say that if you can't measure it, you can't manage it, a costly myth." Part of this sentence has been paraphrased numerous times, and although the meaning has been somewhat misinterpreted, it is correctly attributed to the writer. Edwards Deming is right of course, the paraphrase cannot be ubiquitously applied, the principle is fallible. However, based on many years of running complex operations it is a statement of undeniable fact to say that in order to optimise operational output and maximise productivity in any fast-paced logistics operation (irrespective of the service being provided) it is essential that management teams are largely data-led in their key decision making. Without accurately understanding current operational activity via data generated from pertinent KPIs (key performance indicators), decision making and resulting operational productivity will be sub-optimal. "Shooting from the hip" may work on occasionally or be relevant for simple day-to-day decision making, if the maker is experienced and the problem mundane and straightforward; but, key decisions require robust data not anecdote or guesswork, and forward planning requires science not a hunch.

KPIs are fundamental to successfully managing any operation and or business, and where KPIs are not deployed, when first introduced, the initial data will create the current "baseline" and thereafter the KPI will be the tool that enables a management team to measure improvement, or regression in

DOI: 10.4324/9781003323822-8

operational performance from the baseline. It is not possible to continually improve operational performance without being data-led and KPI-driven; but, a prerequisite is that the data used to formulate KPIs must be accurate and evidenced. However, the leaner the suite of KPIs, the better and avoid creating KPI "overload" which generates a snowstorm of data through which management cannot "see the wood for the trees." The watchword word is KEY in KPI.

Route-based businesses with depot infrastructures deploying LCV/HGV fleets will share common operational characteristics, the service performed at the customer location may differ, but the logistics principles used to get drivers from A to B will be similar, and many management disciplines harmonious. This chapter therefore provides a basic suite of guideline KPIs (key performance indicators) that can be applied and that will provide management teams with core operational data that will directly inform decision making and will aid improved service and enhance productivity. Each business may need to tweak these KPIs to reflect the nuance of the business, and some KPIs will have more or less relevance, for example measuring driver attrition is important in many businesses with LCV fleets, as driver pay is relatively low and attrition high, and the business finds itself having to compete aggressively to recruit and retain staff; but in businesses deploying highly trained and qualified HGV Tanker drivers for example, where salaries are upper-quartile and attrition is stable and low, this KPI will have less relevance as an "anchor" KPI.

In businesses where KPIs have been previously absent, data gathering may be burdensome initially with the requisite data needing to be "hand-cranked" in order to populate the KPI, but over time the business may be able to generate more data automatically via core systems, but if data does need to be derived "long-hand," it is strongly recommended that this should deter or prevent the data being captured. The alternative is to rely on anecdote, intuition, and guesswork to inform decision making and this can only lay a ponderous path to delivering sub-optimal output.

There are four sets of KPIs provided in this chapter, each set covering a separate management discipline, but all 32 KPIs are focused on delivering service excellence to customers, the welfare of colleagues, or operationally productivity. The categories encompass:

- Nine Service KPIs (measuring the provision and quality of service and customer complaints)
- Eight Fleet KPIs (commercial vehicles)

- Ten People (driver)-related KPIs
- Five Health and Safety (specifically related to operational departments)

There is a fifth KPI set which is incorporated into Chapter 12 ("The Depot Manager Cadre") which discusses the benefits of introducing a bonus scheme for depot managers, and if such a scheme is introduced what specific KPIs (just seven KPIs selected from the 32 KPIs outlined above) are best suited to measure depot manager (DM) performance. These KPIs seven are highlighted in the far right-hand column of each figure outlining the four KPI sets.

The other two far right-hand columns indicate the frequency with which the KPI should be published and which managers or management teams should be involved in reviewing.

- The daily drumbeat management call (for further reference, see Chapter 9) will take place each working day and the relevant KPI results published prior to and in readiness for the meeting/call, with exceptions discussed.
- Weekly calls or meetings including senior management.

The nine KPIs in Figure 8.1 focus on customer service and productivity, three are related to complaints and should be viewed in conjunction with the complaints management process outlined in Chapter 7, "Managing Complaints". Each KPI with an * denotes those KPIs which depot teams should have the wherewithal to generate the data "long-hand" to populate the KPI in the absence of the business being capable of produce automatically via the core operating system.

The data source for these KPIs may emanate from various departments (i.e., complaints are most likely to be raised via customer services) and in businesses with sophisticated core systems a greater proportion of base data may be extracted automatically via PDAs, telematics, and software scheduling systems (Figure 8.2).

Fleet KPIs are most likely to be collated and generated by the central fleet management team with data support required on a timely basis from depots, for example, number of hires and spares in depot, vehicles off road (VOR) figures as a check for fleet with third-parties, the number of vehicle incidents and accidents. The six fleet KPIs categorised as "drumbeat" are recommended inclusion at the daily operating rhythm call and results discussed as these reflect elements which directly impact the depot's ability to function

Category	The KPI	Commentary	RAG Drumbeat	RAG week, period & YTD	RAG DM Bonus
Service	% of scheduled drops completed	Target 99%. To be measured at individual driver level, per depot, region and nationally each working day, with summary weekly, period and YTD performance.	✓	✓	
Service*	% of daily contracted / required drops completed	Target 96-98%. The business TBC. The internal target should be greater % than is contracted with customers. To be measured at depot, region and nationally each working day, with summary weekly, period and YTD performance. An anchor KPI usually shared with major customers by customer, and across all customers as a company national average.	✓	✓	✓
Service*	Drops per driver day	Target TBC by business but linked directly with scheduling teams. This target will differ by depot depending on route density and average miles between drops. Measured by driver, depot, region and nationally. Increase target incrementally over time.	✓	✓	
Service*	Drops per hour worked	Target TBC by business but linked directly to scheduling. This target will differ by depot depending on route density and average miles between drops. Measured by driver, depot, region and nationally.	✓	✓	
Service	No. of first time drops not completed that are >3 days late	Each day "scheduled" to include today's contracted and "catch-up" drops from previous day(s) plus ad-hoc and special requests. It is important as a "check-KPI" that any contracted first-time drops missed are identified by schedulers and recovered next day.	✓	✓	
Service*	No. of drops contracted but not routed	The target must be zero. All contracted drops must be scheduled daily and with a realistic probability of being completed, but this is an important check-KPI to warn senior management of an early "red-flag".	✓	✓	
Service	No. of complaints raised	A basic KPI with the target number TBC by the business but will be related to depot drops, Fleet number and complexity of services.	✓	✓	
Service	Ratio of complaints raised against Depot over completed drops	The anchor Complaint KPI. Target TBC by business but a guideline target is complaint numbers to trend @ sub 0.05% of total completed drops.	✓	✓	✓
Service	Number of complaints issued to Depot not resolved in 3+ days	Target zero. This "check KPI" provides a red-flag to senior management if Depot teams are failing to keep pace with inbound customer failures		✓	

Figure 8.1 Guideline service and complaint related KPIs. Note: for further complaint KPIs, refer to Chapter 7.

Category	The KPI	Commentary	RAG Drumbeat	RAG week, period & YTD	RAG DM Bonus
Fleet	Up-time	Target min 96%. Calculated as total Fleet * working days in period over the total number of VOR days in period. This is an anchor KPI, the better the uptime the less reliance on Hire and better customer service	✓	✓	✓
Fleet	+72 hour rule	Target sub 8% of all VOR. The number & % of VOR that are in garage for more than 72 hours (3 working days). This KPI if managed robustly ensures no unwarranted garage delays and keeps Fleet management focused on knowing the exact status of every VOR.	✓	✓	
Fleet*	Number of non-peak hires	Target zero. Excluding planned additional Hire days to meet predicted peaks, this KPI will flag any unnecessary hire that is lingering at depot.	✓	✓	
Fleet*	Number of vehicles submitted late to service / inspection	Target zero. Depots have an important role to play in achieving 96%+ uptime, and one essential DM task is to ensure release of vehicles on-time and to schedule for services and planned inspections.	✓	✓	
Fleet*	Number of RTAs / incidents	Target TBC by business, but rachet target 6-monthly. The number and severity need to be reported daily to ensure senior management are aware of serious incidents, DMs to trend problematic drivers, and depot performance is published to provide early warning of issues.	✓	✓	✓
Fleet*	Speeding events (telematics)	Target. 0.5 speeding events by driver by day. Associated and provided with Telematics. Monitoring speeding incident trends will reduce fuel consumption, reduce accidents, incidents and driver lost-time.	✓	✓	
Fleet	Miles per drop	Target TBC by business. Link with scheduling. The aim is to improve trends over time & reduce the average MPD as density and scheduling efficiency improves. Comparative results between depots with similar geographical and demographic areas.			✓
Fleet	Miles per gallon	Target TBC. Measure at vehicle, model type, depot, region and nationally. Good indicator of vehicle mechanical problems and or poor driving standards and potentially drive fuel theft. Link to telematic reports.			✓

Figure 8.2 Guideline fleet KPIs. Note: Tachograph related KPIs are excluded but will need inclusion where HGV fleet exist.

on the day and deliver customer service or represent a potential red flag as to surplus costs (number of hires in depot).

Of the people KPIs (Figure 8.3) arguably the attrition rate is the most important (unless the driver is trending at sub-20%) as the output of this KPI influences the results of several other KPIs. Colleagues leave a business for many reasons, some of which are beyond the control of management (e.g. retirement, betterment, relocation or applying a skill in another role and which is not required in the business); however, the "revolving door" syndrome of new starters constantly leaving in less than six months can be debilitating to a business, hence the criticality of this KPI. Elevated levels of short-term attrition also increase business training and recruitment costs, consume depot management team time through continuous interviewing and inducting new starters, and during the induction period new employees are performing at sub-optimum productivity and therefore depot output is inhibited and service quality negatively impacted.

The people KPIs are all related to managing depots in a structured and professional manner, they focus on factors that, if not controlled robustly, are likely to result in service inefficiency and increased costs, many of these elements are discussed in Chapter 1 ("People Management") (Figure 8.4).

Category	The KPI	Commentary	RAG Drumbeat	RAG week, period & YTD	RAG DM Bonus
People	% Attrition rate	TBC by business. An Anchor KPI. A guideline target is <30% for unqualified (non HGV) driving staff and <20% for qualified / HGV. Measure on rolling 3 & 13 month trend basis. Poor attrition will increase training & recruitment costs.	✓		✓
People	Attrition stability index	Target 85%+. This is the measure of the % of employees with + 1 year service (also measure +3, 5 & 10 years), it indicates if a "revolving-door" syndrome is occurring with recent-starters so measure year 1 in quarter periods.		✓	
People*	Absence & sickness %	Target <3%. Measure to colleague, Depot, Region and nationally. Sickness & absence trends will be higher in inner cities and lower in rural areas. An anchor KPI.	✓	✓	✓
People*	Establishment planned vs. actual	Target to maintain Actual heads to within <3% of the agreed Establishment by period. If the gap widens it is likely to increase OT and agency costs (the latter will impact Fleet costs) and negatively impact customer service.	✓	✓	
People*	% Holidays taken	Target maximum 10%, minimum 7%, with period average @ 8%. Measured at driver, depot, region and nationally. A anchor KPI. Calculation total sickness and absence days in period over total worked days (excluding holidays and worked weekends)	✓	✓	
People*	% Holidays remaining not taken	Target each period from P1 – P12 to consume min 8% taken therefore target a decreasing counter %. For example, P1 = 92%, P2 = 84%, P3 = 76% and so on. The business may want to flex an annual plan to take peak holiday or planned "down-time" (if business has a known low point in trading volume) into account.		✓	
People*	OT hours %	TBC by business. The budget may flex the plan per period to taken peak trading into account. This is an anchor KPI as OT is paid at 1+ time so every hour increases labour costs without improving productivity, indeed the converse may be evident as colleague fatigue occurs if individuals that work long OT hours continually.	✓	✓	
People*	Paid hours vs. budgeted / planned	Target zero variance, unless new growth not budgeted impacts actual hours. This is an "anchor" KPI which is impacted by how efficiently other people KPIs are managed.		✓	
People*	Agency hours	Target TBC. Measure in hours / days and as a % (similar to OT). A key KPI as every hour is usually more expensive than an employee but output likely much less.	✓	✓	
People*	Under-worked hours	Target zero. This KPI measures the variance between hours actually worked and paid. They should logically be identical but regrettably it often is not, it reflects poor processes and represents wasted time and costs, and root-cause must be corrected.	✓	✓	

Figure 8.3 Guideline people (driving colleague) related KPIs.

Category	The KPI	Commentary	RAG Drumbeat	RAG week, period & YTD	RAG DM Bonus
Health & Safety	No. of Riddors*	Target zero. A Riddor is a lost time incident of 7 days or skeletal fracture, or worse. Every Riddor should result in formal investigation (see H&S Chapter 11). Measured by Depot, Region & Nationally weekly, period & YTD	✓	✓	✓
Health & Safety	Number of lost-time* incidences (less than Riddor)	To include Drivers and all other depot employees. Targets TBC by business, this KPI should focus on improving trends continually over time.	✓	✓	
Health & Safety	Number of near-misses* raised	TBC by each business but as a guideline each Depot (of +10 drivers) should be raising 3 per week as a minimum average if the H&S culture is internalised.		✓	
Health & Safety	Audit (internal) result completed in week	Large businesses will have an internal H&S and possibly Environmental Officer / and team, if so H&S depot audits must be conducted with a program of audits and any "red-flags" escalated in the week of audit and root-cause corrected.		✓	
Health & Safety	Notification of visit from the HSE*	This is a check-KPI and early warning of a potential to senior management therefore DMs should escalate on the drumbeat call if aware.	✓	✓	

Figure 8.4   Guideline anchor H&S KPIs relating to operational depots.

Health and safety (H&S) has a dedicated chapter (Chapter 11), but a basic suite of operational H&S KPIs are incorporated to provide a rounded pack for operational management. Front and centre of management thinking must be the health and safety of all colleagues; a fundamental objective rarely discussed, but which has traumatic consequences for everyone involved, and which has a lasting impact, is the basic goal to get every driver that commences work each to return safely to the depot and get home to their family. During covid (2021 statistics), there are on average five people killed on the road daily (this figure is down 11% on prior year)[1], no operations manager wants one of their colleagues becoming a statistic.

Of the five KPIs, arguably the most important is the notification of a Reporting of Injuries, Diseases and Dangerous Occurrences Regulations (RIDDOR)[2] and at the earliest time feasible post incident, but every RIDDOR or potential RIDDOR incident should feature on the daily operating rhythm call to ensure notification, understand if support or further action is required, by whom and by when. The senior operations management team and Head of/Manager of Health and Safety need to be alerted of a potential RIDDOR on the day of the incident and as soon as is practical.

Balance Scorecard

When evaluating depot performance in a holistic way, it can be useful to collate a number of anchor KPIs together and design a depot "Balance Scorecard"[3] to provide a balanced picture of depot overall performance, but which serves a comparative mechanism (see Figure 8.5). The two core

Balance Scorecard for Depot X								(example row assumes that period results reference P3, with a depot driver establishment of 30, and target drops per driver day of 31)						
	service		*productivity*		*people management*				*resources*			*complaints*		*health & safety*
KPI	% drops completed over planned	% drops completed over planned	Drops per driver day	Drops per driver day	% of absence	% of holiday taken	% of OT	% of hours worked but not paid	Budged driver headcount	Variance to budged driver headcount	% attrition 13 months	% complaints over total drops	% complaints over total drops	No. of RIDDORS	No. of RIDDORS
Time frame	Period	YTD	Period	YTD	Period	Period	Period	Period	Period	Period	Period	Period	YTD	Period	YTD
Guideline target	98%	98%	31	31	<3%	8%	12%	<1%	30	zero	<20%	<0.05%	<0.05%	zero	zero
Example	98.4%	97.0%	32	30	4.0%	8.4%	15%	2%	29	-1	22.0%	0.035%	0.05%	0	1
RAG	Yes	Yes	Yes	Yes	Yes	Yes	Yes	Yes	No	Yes	Yes	Yes	Yes	Yes	Yes

Figure 8.5   An example depot Balance Scorecard compiled from ten "anchor" KPIs.

objectives (colleague H&S aside) for a depot management team are to strive to achieve the contractual service level agreements (SLAs) (this guarantees service performance to contract), this percentage target will differ by business but is likely to be in the range of 96%–99%, and to achieve the optimum average completed drops/services per route which is primary productivity measure.

In Figure 8.5, the numbers/percentages given in row named "Example" are for illustrative purposes only, incorporating a RAG status immediately draws the eye to those elements that are sub-target. The numbers/percentages in row "Guideline target" reflect commonly applied targets; however, each business will need to determine targets that specifically suit their business environment.

The depot scorecard provides a data platform that the DM and his or her line manager can review periodically (recommended once each month or financial reporting period). There is likely to be positive and negative results displayed unless the target setting was initially not challenging enough, the aim after all, is not to have a 100% green RAGGED scoreboard, the aim is to continually improve productivity and output whilst sustaining service at or better than the SLA, and integral to a culture that seeks to always push the boundaries of performance, it would be natural for some scorecard KPIs to fluctuate through RAG.

Basic Depot "Trading" (Periodic Financial Review)

Companies vary in the way that they view and treat depots from a financial perspective, some consider them profit centres and others less complex cost centres. In businesses that provide national services and that have nationwide customers, accurate allocation of revenue per depot (and specifically to mirror the depot's geographical service area) can prove to be problematic, and businesses with many thousands of customers may find that the internal cost and time to accurately apportion customer revenue by depot is greater than the benefit of doing so. The author has worked in a business that has allocated revenue by depot, and not entirely accurately, and it fosters an environment where DMs spent a disproportionate amount of their time at each month-end of course, and ultimately influenced the DM's bonus potential) rather than their primary focus and reason for being, which are the core tasks of improving operational productivity and delivering to the SLA.

It is essential that DMs have at least a cost budget for their depot, and this budget must incorporate customer volume, depicted either in drops or services, and if the business service is segmented into a unit of some description, the volume budget (annual forward plan) should include both the average expected number of drops and units per month. This will prove invaluable when analysing operational ratios (for example, average units per drop, or average drops per route), actual vs. plan. Where a business has not had depot budgeting previously, the first full year must be viewed as a pilot year, there will inevitably be errors and inconsistencies, but as the year unfolds both Finance and Operational teams will learn a great deal about the business and what works operationally, by the mid-point of year one meaningful discussions will be taking place and both service and productivity improve and the quality of decision making become sharper as it will be ever more influenced by meaningful and accurate data.

At its most basic, DMs and their teams need to appreciate that every overtime hour, every absence day, every vehicle damage incident, every credit given to customer for missed delivery has a cost, and every management decision has a cost consequence.

Large businesses with sophisticated core systems will have structured financial reporting systems and a myriad of metrics, and for managers working in such environments this section is not going to add value; but if the reader is working in a business with no depot financial reporting or limited financial data, the following tables may prove illuminating. Figure 8.6 provides an example of the data sources that require collation each month in order for management to understand the variable labour costs at a depot, and which will provide an insight into the positive and negative impact each cost line can have on overall labour depot cost and how the various elements influence each other.

Depot X	P1	P1	P1	P1	
Number of working days	22		RAG		Commentary
Drivers (labour)	Budget	Actual	Variance	% Var	
Number of Drops	17,600	17,700	100	0.6%	Completed drops (services) are required not planned drops
Number of units.	61600	60180	1420	2.3%	If the business measures units (individual products as a sub-categiories deployed at each drop it is important to capture this data)
Average units per drop	3.5	3.4	-0.1	-2.9%	Total units / total drops (the latter will be the smaller number)
Establishment	32	30	-2	-6.3%	Establishment equals the budgeted driver headcount in period
Overtime percentage	11%	19%	-8%		An important measure, as OT is paid at 1+ time so measuring actual versus plan is essential. In this example OT costs have risen due to headcount shortage. The % is measured as OT hrs over total paid hrs.
Basic pay (contracted hours)	£54,208	£49,755	£4,453	8.2%	Contracted standard weekly hours (in the example 40 hours per week at a rate of £11.00). Headcount is -2 (6%) hence the "improvement"
Overtime pay	£7,800	£13,808	-£6,008	-77.0%	Reduced headcount has resulted in higher OT to meet volume demand
Agency driver pay	£0	£0	£0	0.0%	Some businesses may use agency labour, if so it must be measured
Bank holiday pay.	£0.0	£0.0	£0.0		An important sub category, in the example Period 1 has no B.H.
Holiday pay.	£5,808	£5,808.0	£0.0	0.0%	Holiday pay warrants measurement, if holidays are not robustly managed period results can be adversely impacted
Sickness & absence pay.	£1,936	£2,581.0	-£645.0	-33.3%	Essential to measure. Increased absence has impacted the period result
Total pay	£69,752	£71,952	-£2,200	-3.2%	The sum of all individual labour cost lines
Total pay + N.I. & pension	£79,517	£82,026	-£2,508	-3.2%	Total pay plus National insurance & pension (@ 14% in the example)
Holiday % taken	8%	8%	0%		Reference "People Management" for more detailed explanation
Holiday % outstanding	92%	92%	0%		
Sickness & absence %	3%	4.5%	-1.5%		Reference "People Management" for more detailed explanation
Ave. labour cost per drop	£4.52	£4.63	-£0.12	-2.6%	*Per drop / unit averages provide comparative labour*
Ave. labour cost per unit	£1.29	£1.36	-£0.07	-5.6%	*metrics across all depots*

Figure 8.6   An example of the minimum data elements that require recording monthly to produce a basic financial understanding of employee costs at a depot.

Figure 8.6 shows an example of the minimum data elements that require recording monthly to produce a basic financial understanding of employee costs at a depot.

It is important for DMs to focus on "controlling the controllable"[4] and avoid being distracted with fixed cost elements that in reality the DM has little or zero influence over, and which have no relevance to his or her primary objectives, for example: Rent, rates, and utility costs, or nationally procured functions including depot repairs and maintenance, premises cleaning, and depot security. Focus on consumables and equipment is pertinent as they are related to service and may be liable to damage and or internal theft, these need reviewing on a business-by-business case as to whether they warrant inclusion in the labour model.

Figure 8.7 provides a similarly basic model for fleet and fuel costs.

In order to complete the table in Figure 8.7, operational managers will need the collaboration and support of the Financial Department, some of this data will not be readily accessible to depot or perhaps even senior

Depot X	P1	P1	P1	P1	
Number of working days	22		RAG		Commentary
Fleet & Fuel	Budget	Actual	Variance	% Var	
Number of Drops	17,600	17,700	100	0.6%	Completed drops (services), not planned drops which is a higher number
Number of miles driven	105600	108350	-2750	-2.6%	Total miles driven across all vehicle routes in the period
Number of RTAs & incidences	1	3	-2	-200%	Number of road accidents or vehicle damage incidents (i.e; reverse parking) in the period
Number of hire vehicles	0	0	0	0.0%	Number of vehicle charged hire days in the period divided by the number of working days in period (22 in P1)
Fleet Establishment	33	33	0	0.0%	No. of company commercial vehicles based at Depot in the period including spares
Cost of hire vehicles	£0	£0	£0	0%	Cost of vehicle hire days & all related hire damage & other costs
Fleet depreciation	£8,000	£8,000	£0	0.0%	Fleet depreciation (in example 20 of 33 vehicles, over 60 months)
Fleet lease costs	£6,240	£6,450	-£210	-3.4%	Lease costs (including all R&M for 13 lease vehicles), higher in-period costs reflect driver damage in the period.
R&M costs	£1,800.0	£1,625.0	£175.0	9.7%	R&M (repair & maintenance)associated with 20 Depreciated vehicles.
Accident & damage costs	£500	£2,250.0	-£1,750.0	-350.0%	Accident / incident repair costs associated with three RTAs / incidents above
Breakdown & recovery	£180	£0.0	£180.0	100.0%	Recovery of any breakdown or accident vehicle and transport to garage
Fuel Cost	£20,559	£19,286	£1,272.7	6.2%	Total in period fuel cost
Total Fleet cost	£37,279	£37,611	-£332	-0.9%	
Fuel litres consumed	19580	18908	672	3.4%	Actual litres consumed related to total miles driven, in the example the budget was 24 mpg, the actual Fleet due to robust Telematics management, and good dcolleague driving, delivered 25.5 mpg
Fuel cost	£20,559	£19,286	£1,273	6.2%	Actual pence per litre was a postive 2 pence lower than budgeted
Average cost per accident	£500.00	£750.00	-£250.00	-50.0%	The number of incidents vs. budget was higher in ratio terms than the average cost per inceident as two of the three were low damage incidents
Average Fleet p.p.mile	35.3	34.7	0.6	1.7%	
Average miles per drop	6.0	6.1	0.1	1.7%	

Figure 8.7   A basic fleet and fuel financial reporting data set.

operations managers, for example vehicle and MHE hire invoice costs, vehicle breakdown and recovery invoices, and accident and repair charges from suppliers. Lease costs are straightforward to populate once the data is shared from the finance team. The fleet manager and or team is also going to be actively involved to collating and providing some of this information, once the template is created and being populated, it will be most rewarding if representatives from the three departments (Operations, Fleet, and Finance) jointly review output on a monthly basis and together determine the "direction of travel" regarding depot performance and actions arising from a collaborative decision-making process and for the DM and the team to make to continually improve performance. The suggested participants at the monthly review meeting would include

Operations	Depot Manager, Regional Manager, and or COO
Fleet	Head of Fleet
Finance	Finance partner to Operations or CFO

Notes

1. Reported road casualties in GB, provision estimates year ending June 2021. Roadacc.stats@dft.gov.uk.
2. Health and Safety Executive. www.hse.gov.uk/riddor/.
3. Norton, D. P., & Kaplan, R. S. 1996. *The Balanced Scorecard: Translating Strategy into Action.* Boston, MA: Harvard Business School Press; Norton, D. P., & Kaplan, R. S. 2000. *The Strategy Focused Organisation.* Boston, MA: Harvard Business School Press.
4. Medcalf, J., & Gilbert, J. 2015. *Transformational Leadership.* Fishpond.

Chapter 9

The Management Operating Rhythm (Drumbeat)

Introduction

Route-based high-volume service companies present challenging, busy operational environments with multiple "moving-parts" and even with the best forward planning teams may not have a ready solution for every operational obstacle that might arise, for example vehicle breakdown, a road traffic accident (RTA), unannounced employee absences, snow, flooding or other inclement weather event, an urgent customer request, or even the occasional power cut caused by a cable being inadvertently severed by a road-working team in close proximity to the depot. To maintain service excellence at optimum cost in such a volatile environment demands absolute focus from every operational manager, and to maintain uninterrupted pace operationally to execute the daily service plan, whilst dealing with the unexpected demands calm control, an experienced hand at the tiller, and importantly an overarching communication structure spanning operations that provide pertinent and timely data to inform and enable management to determine the best course of action operationally.

A robust communication structure reinforces the need to execute essential operational tasks and processes whilst being responsive to operational obstacles requiring support and or an activity change to resolve. Figure 9.1 provides a guideline "operating rhythm" comprising structured calls and or meetings that will ensure business operational momentum is maintained and

DOI: 10.4324/9781003323822-9

Meeting / Call	When	Who	Why

Operations Drumbeat call (target 30 minutes)	Daily (working day)	• Regional management (each Region may conduct a separate call or one call is convening nationally)
		• DMs (or 2IC if the DM is on leave)
		• Senior Fleet manager or 2IC
		• Scheduling senior team (split regionally if appropriate)
		• Attending once per week, or as invited:
		  • COO once per week or for pertinent updates or as stand-in if one RM is on leave
		  • H&S senior manager
		  • Customer services (Head of dept.)
		  • Sales Heads (update on new business)
		  • Others (e.g. for business announcements)
			1. Gather Ops depot DMs together to review YESTERDAY'S performance (by exception) and reasons for failures.
			2. To understand pinch-points impacting TODAY'S planned service and discuss / agree resolution.
			3. Flag any stock, equipment, Fleet issues TODAY and discuss resolution among DMs and wider supporting Ops functions.
			4. To ensure all service and other key metric administrative tasks are up to date & accurate as this data feeds many other reports.
			5. To enable the RM / COO to brief their teams of wider business issues.
			6. To discuss customer key issues and formulate areas for future planning (i.e. Christmas & other Bank-holidays)
			7. To provide Sales, Customer service, H&S etc. a once per week platform to update generally or an "emergency" platform at short notice.

Weekly senior team KPI review	Weekly	• COO (Operations Director) • RMs • Heads of Fleet & scheduling • Operations analyst	1. To review all KPI trends as a team for the week and YTD by Depot, Region and Nationally and agree actions to ensure continual improvement. To determine what support / action is required if any Depot is displaying early signs of service or other challenge.
Weekly scheduling productivity review	Weekly	• RM with DMs attending individually to schedule • Head of scheduling + planners to schedule	1. To conduct a detailed review per Depot to ensure that both Planner / DM are, together, extracting optimum benefit, and if not agree what mechanisms / tasks are required going forward, with accountability, time-line and what support is required and by who.
Fleet accidents review	Once per period	• COO (Operations Director) • Selected DMs with worse accident record. • Head of Fleet plus RM relevant to attending DM	1. Reference Chapter 2 – Fleet Management 2. To ensure the post accident investigations are meticulously conducted, review learnings and ensure resulting actions were appropriate and being progressed in a timely fashion.
Riddor review meeting	Once per period	• COO (Operations Director) • Head of H&S plus appropriate RM • Individually and to schedule, each DM with RIDDOR	1. Reference Chapter 11 – Health & Safety 2. To ensure each investigation was properly and thoroughly conducted, learnings endorsed, and ensure appropriate actions taken. Understand legal implications and senior support required.
Complaints review meeting	Once per period	• COO + RMs • Head of customer service + complaints administrator • Depot DMs with worse complaints ratios	1. Reference Chapter 7 – Complaint Management 2. To review Complaint performance per Depot and holistically to understand trends, root-causes and potential Depot challenges.

Figure 9.1   Guideline monthly operating rhythm call/meeting schedule.

is a platform for promoting adherence to common company processes and procedures.

Anyone who has played sport or is an avid professional sports fan will appreciate the importance of structured communication, it is the glue that binds teams together and ensures the collective moves forward as a uniform entity without inhibiting individuals to perform at their best.

The six meetings/calls outlined in Figure 9.1 reflect the core suite of meetings that enable senior operational managers and depot managers (DMs) to work in a unified way and to be data-led. These meetings envelope the critical elements required to manage operational matters effectively and ensure that focus on customer service does not deviate irrespective of what internal or external challenge arises. These meetings are "cast in stone," fixed in everyone's diary for the year ahead with management attendance mandatory, the only permitted reason for absence being holiday or sickness, and on these occasions the absent participant's second in command at depot (2IC) is automatically planned to attend and to be fully prepared with requisite data.

Each attendee is expected to attend on time and fully "armed" with the relevant data that they present or be cognisant of, and that data will be accurate, current, and pertinent. Of the six meetings/calls, the most important is the daily "drumbeat" call, this reflects the heartbeat of the operation.

The drumbeat call will be held each morning at the earliest time feasible to ensure that issues inhibiting service that day can be aired and discussed on the call with time to facilitate resolution, that said, standard operating irritations at depot (non-starting vehicles, absence, loading bay not working, etc.) would be expected to be handled resolutely by the DM and the team and fully resolved before the call takes place. The call is most helpful to conduct once most of the daily routes are on the road. The first priority in the morning for the DM is to muster the operation (see Chapter 4, "Minimising Non-productive Hours"), but from experience, most despatch operations take place in a 05.00–08.00 window, and with this timeline in mind, as a guideline, the author would usually conduct the daily drumbeat call at 08.00 hours, with an expected duration of 30 minutes subject to all participants being fully prepared, but in practice, the time of the drumbeat call will be unique to each business.

To glean maximum benefit from the call, accurate and complete data is required regarding yesterday's service performance by depot, and full knowledge of every route, vehicle condition, and driver colleagues' attendance and absence regarding today's operation must be understood in detail by each DM. No apology for repeating "the bleeding obvious," to coin a Monty Python sketch, preparation and accurate data is the cornerstone of the drumbeat call. It is not a chat show and avoid permitting anecdote and "I think so," or "I'll get back to you after the call," professional managers on top of their game will know their data and want to know it and take pride in demonstrating their ability and expertise on the drumbeat call with their peer group.

In a turnaround situation, or when implementing a structured communications process (including the drumbeat call) where none has previously existed, as COO, I would initially chair the drumbeat call to establish a standard process, the pace, and instil the need to attend fully briefed, but once the process had settled into a smooth but meticulous operating mode, the RMs would chair small groups in their individual drumbeat calls with the COO attending each call once per week, on a set day, to provide a brief high-level update or to answer any specific operational or business question.

The three "review" calls (Fleet, RIDDOR, and Complaints) are discussed in detail in the relevant chapter, the senior KPI review meeting is conducted weekly and enables senior management to take the time each week to reflect upon the performance of individual depot teams using the depot Balance Scorecard together with other KPI data (Chapter 8 "KPIs, the Balance Scorecard, and Basic Financial Models"), with the aim of identifying any pertinent trends or potential "red flags" and to determine relevant actions, investigations, or additional support (why, who, what, and when) for the DM and or the team that might improve performance.

The weekly scheduling review is a regional meeting designed to bring together the DM, the local planner, the Head of Scheduling (if the role exists), and RM in order to analyse in detail the scheduling and actual service delivery performance of each depot in granular detail to understand the reason why specific drivers, routes, or depots are underperforming relative to peers and discuss and agree what tasks and actions can be taken, by who and when, and with what support if any, to arrest or enhance performance. Targets for incremental improvement will be established with and reviewed weekly going forward. This meeting is a platform where DMs and planners might take learnings from their colleagues and a forum for sharing good practice.

Chapter 10

Operational Health and Safety

Introduction

Health and safety (H&S) management is a science and management discipline in its own right and there have been many books written on the topic; therefore, this chapter focuses on operational health and safety and is deliberately "light-touch" but worthy of inclusion, some smaller businesses have little or no health and safety contingent and the content herein may prove helpful. In route-based service sector businesses, operational departments are likely to encompass the majority of employees and many of these employees will be driving commercial vehicles daily, with most company accidents and incidents most likely to affect operational personnel and be vehicle related.

Colleague health and safety is the top priority of management, whilst this book examines methodologies to improve productivity; working safely and legally is paramount, and colleagues' well-being must be at the heart of every procedure, process, and task that management teams lead. Operational managers must personally own and be accountable for the health and safety of their colleagues, it is not simply the responsibility of the H&S manager, many companies will not have this role, it is a fundamental part of the depot manager's role, and they must be fully conversant with H&S legislation. When managers have genuine accountability for health and safety practices, then colleagues are also more likely to buy into the need to act and think "safety" with due regard to themselves and for others around them when performing their duties. Often the H&S management team (if there is one) in a business is lean and thinly spread geographically and their

DOI: 10.4324/9781003323822-10

Category	The KPI	Commentary	RAG Drumbeat	RAG week, period & YTD	RAG DM Bonus
Health & Safety	No. of Riddors*	Target zero. A Riddor is a lost time incident of 7 days or skeletal fracture, or worse. Every Riddor should result in formal investigation (see H&S Chapter 11). Measured by Depot, Region & Nationally weekly, period & YTD	✓	✓	✓
Health & Safety	Number of lost-time* incidences (less than Riddor)	To include Drivers and all other depot employees. Targets TBC by business, this KPI should focus on improving trends continually over time.	✓	✓	
Health & Safety	Number of near-misses* raised	TBC by each business but as a guideline each Depot (of +10 drivers) should be raising 3 per week as a minimum average if the H&S culture is internalised.			✓
Health & Safety	Audit (internal) result completed in week	Large businesses will have an internal H&S and possibly Environmental Officer / and team, if so H&S depot audits must be conducted with a program of audits and any "red-flags" escalated in the week of audit and root-cause corrected.			✓
Health & Safety	Notification of visit from the HSE*	This is a check-KPI and early warning of a potential to senior management therefore DMs should escalate on the drumbeat call if aware.	✓	✓	

Figure 10.1   Basic guideline H&S KPIs.

role therefore is fundamentally one of support and mentoring, and to provide technical advice and guidance. There should not be a need for large H&S management contingent if operational management comprehensively internalise and promote good H&S practice, but in order to achieve this outcome, senior business leadership must internalise this philosophy and invest in requisite training of depot managers to provide them with the training and education they require to fulfil their role.

Figure 10.1 was also included in Chapter 8 as part of the core suite of key performance indicators (KPIs) recommended for a route-based business. If the business has a health and safety manager, then these KPIs (and likely many more) will probably already form part of the business monitoring and reporting processes and therefore this set may be discounted. The top three KPIs in the table are essentially trend metrics, the objective is to achieve incremental improvement over time from the base position (the respective number or percentage at the point of initial data collation) rather than seeking a specific target number; however, it is possible to compare business actual results to industry standards and to use the standard as a minimum target to achieve.[1]

Near Miss Reporting

The Safety Triangle[2] is a cornerstone of H&S measurement and whilst some observers question the validity of the ratios used, fundamentally the concept is sound. Measuring, monitoring, and instilling an expectation across all colleagues the principle of continually increasing the number of near miss notifications will reduce the number of lost-time incidents. However, in order to achieve a meaningful reduction in lost-time incidents each near miss needs to be recorded diligently, the root cause determined, and the learnings understood locally by the depot management team in order that they can share these learning with colleagues via a toolbox talk; otherwise, near miss reporting may become a superficial administration exercise to appease senior management rather than a meaningful process and one which will genuinely reduce the rate and number of incidents.

LTIFR

The lost-time injury frequency rate (LTIFR)[3] is a useful measure and whilst it does not differentiate between levels of severity, it is nonetheless a meaningful indicator, which will over time enable the business and senior management to gauge trend improvement, the calculation is:

$$\frac{\text{The number of lost} - \text{time incidents} * 1,000,000}{\text{Number of hours worked by employees during the period}}$$

The metric is best reported each financial reporting period (whether four-weekly or calendar month) with actual monthly results vs. target and additionally applying a rolling three- and 13-month reporting picture.

RIDDOR

It is a legal requirement[4] to report every Reporting of Injuries, Diseases and Dangerous Occurrences Regulations (RIDDOR) incident (a lost-time incident of seven days, or an incident involving a bone fracture or worse injury or fatality at work), and serious incidents may incur a visit from the governmental Health and Safety Executive (HSE) department and could result in subsequent investigation. Measuring and reporting RIDDOR incidents internally within the business is essential and is a legal obligation, so this is an anchor KPI. Targeting a reducing (improving) number of RIDDOR incidents each year as an Operations team will help focus attention on the need to minimise the number of RIDDOR events and it is the "acid-test" of a business's H&S record, especially as route-based businesses have large numbers of employees actively involved daily in both driving and ergonomic tasks.

RIDDOR Management Periodic Reviews

In Chapter 9 ("The Management Operating Rhythm (Drumbeat)") the period RIDDOR review is included as one of the key "drumbeat" meetings to reinforce the importance to the business and to ensure that key learnings are understood and cascaded across the organisation, and that the investigation was conducted thoroughly. Each RIDDOR has a negative impact to the business, which may include employee lost-time, insurance claim, and management time (especially if the HSE determine to investigate).

The RIDDOR review meeting presents an opportunity to improve operational processes, procedures, and either vehicle or colleague equipment design if equipment malfunction or failure was contributory to the incident. It is not uncommon for a RIDDOR incident to result in an insurance claim against the company, perhaps reflecting the litigious societal trend of recent times, and in order to protect the business from unsubstantiated claims, it is vital that immediate and meticulous investigation is initiated within 24 hours of each RIDDOR incident, including interviews with the colleague(s) involved, and attaining of signed statements from the injured party(s), any witnesses, and members of the management team conducting the investigation, this can prove invaluable as insurance claims may take weeks or months to culminate and be resolved; and to this end, a periodic (monthly or in line with the business financial calendar) and formal review of each RIDDOR incident that occurred the previous month is highly recommended. In practice, the number to review monthly should be minimal or zero on average if the business operating procedures are robust. Figure 10.2 indicates the participants who should attend the meeting.

The duration of each RIDDOR review need not take more than 30 minutes if the investigation has been completed diligently with the support and involvement (as required) of the H&S and fleet management (if vehicle related) teams as appropriate.

The aim of each review is:

1. To ensure the post investigation was conducted within the guideline target time of 24 working hours (unless a protagonist is absent or hospitalised; however, this party's statement should be the only missing element), and to ensure that the investigation was appropriate and meticulous, if it is deemed that the investigation has shortcomings, the meeting members must identify what subsequent action is needed, by who and to be completed by when, and importantly reconvene a follow-up meeting to ensure progress.

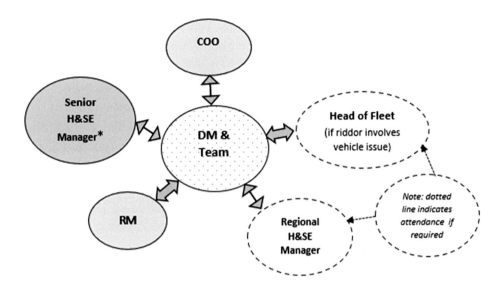

Figure 10.2 contents:
- COO
- Senior H&SE Manager*
- DM & Team
- Head of Fleet (if riddor involves vehicle issue)
- RM
- Regional H&SE Manager
- Note: dotted line indicates attendance if required

Note* In Figure 10.2. the senior H&SE manager is presumed to be the company representative that consults with the business insurance supplier regarding Riddor related insurance claims. if this is not the case the appropriate individual should attend

Figure 10.2   Guideline monthly RIDDOR review meeting with participants.

2. To understand if basic compliance factors were implemented by the depot team regarding the colleague(s) involved in the incident, and this should encompass, but not be limited to:
    a. Previous Training which was provided with all accompanying training records included to review and clarification as to whether said records were duly signed and dated by both management and colleague at the time of training.
    b. The employee was conducting in line with company procedures, in the role that the colleague was performing at time of incident, and the colleague was contracted, trained, and competent to perform the role.
    c. All licence related documents (e.g. driving licence) have been checked and are valid, which means in-date and appropriate to the vehicle being driven.
    d. Working hours and rest periods are in line with company policy and meet legal requirements embracing HGV and LCV rest hours between working shifts, and the working time directive.
    e. The vehicle and or equipment was road-worthy at the time of the incident, in good order and maintained with relevant records

    (i.e., last service or inspection dates, tyre changes and tread-depth, etc.), and the driver daily vehicle check was completed at the start of duty on the day of the incident.

   f. To understand if defect reports were previously raised with a defect likely in any way to be considered directly or indirectly related to the incident (and for the specific vehicle – with dates and timelines specified) and whether they were duly resolved or remain incomplete at time of the incident.

   g. That depot management had attended the scene of the incident (at the same time of the day as the incident occurred if possible) and obtained comprehensive photographic evidence and a thorough appreciation of the environment.

   h. Whether the injured party and witnesses had been interviewed with signed statements secured.

   i. If a vehicle was involved and vehicles off road (VOR) as a result, or the fault was perceived to be a contributory factor, for example brakes, tyres, working parts (doors/shutters); the vehicle was not used subsequently by any other employee, but parked (with keys safely stored) and latterly inspected by a garage, or if a serious incident, the fleet manager may facilitate an independent third-party assessment (e.g. Logistics UK – formerly the FTA) with subsequent report and findings completed. To understand the results from either garage or assessor and determine any next steps.

   j. The employee's record and history has been reviewed to understand if similar previous incidents or accidents have arisen, what the circumstances were, and what previous action if any was taken by management.

3. To understand the root cause of the incident/accident and whether company procedures and or processes were adhered to, and whether these procedures were contributory in any way and therefore would benefit from further examination and improving.

4. To identify learnings (procedural, mechanical, further training) and present solutions for discussion going forward, for example a change to procedures, equipment re-design or upgrade, modifications to training programmes. Future enhancements identified locally are likely to need implementing nationally.

5. To understand what disciplinary action (if warranted) took place or is in progress with a colleague and for what reasons, and does the reviewing team consider this action proportionate?

Driver Assessment and Training

Vehicles are the means to providing customer service in any route-based business, cost significant money, and purchased with an expectation that they will last until fully depreciated or until lease-end. Road traffic accidents (RTAs) do occur and occasionally a vehicle is so irreparably damaged that it is too costly to repair and "written-off." Minor vehicle accidents and damage incidents occur daily, with the root cause rarely mechanical, and virtually always driver related, be it employee or third-party.

Every vehicle related incident may result in a VOR which may negatively impact fleet availability and therefore customer service in addition to the vehicle replacement cost, or repair cost, and any associated colleague overtime costs. A commercial vehicle has the potential to be a killing machine, even a slow speed reversing manoeuvre may fatally injure a member of the public or colleague if the vehicle is poorly driven and without care in densely populated places such as customer carparks, clinics or doctor surgeries, schools, etc.

Therefore, the following health and safety protocols are recommended for consideration:

1. Driver assessor. Each depot with plus 20 vehicles should have a trained driver assessor, a driving colleague that when not assessing is conducting daily service routes as a working driver and to minimise costs, depots with sub-20 vehicles may accommodate an element of sharing one assessor if geography permits. The assessor training course is formal and will need to be conducted by an external professionally qualified and recognised third-party supplier.
2. Reversing in yard. During the final interview stage and before committing to making a job offer, the assessor should conduct structured vehicle manoeuvres with the candidate (these manoeuvres should be common to all depots and designed in conjunction with Head of Fleet) and they must include reserving and parking using cones to assess basic vehicle handling capability.
3. Induction assessor support. During driver induction, the assessor should spend at least two days (not consecutive) in-cab with a new employee to assess driving competency and feedback results to the DM.
4. Telematics and the induction period. Each day during the induction period, the new driver's telematics results (speeding events, harsh acceleration, cornering, and braking) need examination and if there are

early signs of poor driving, the assessor will immediately support and management will consult with the driver to ensure the driver is aware of shortcomings, and if his or her driving performance fails to improve rapidly to a satisfactory and safe standard, the DM must consider whether to curtail the induction.

Vehicle and Equipment Design

When refining the design of an existing vehicle or designing a new fleet vehicle variant and or ancillary equipment, the senior H&S manager should be involved in all such projects from the outset, it is important to optimise ergonomics[5] and apply the MAC tool when considering colleagues' tasks and physical movements and this exercise should incorporate the three points of contact rule[6] for all manual-handling tasks associated with loading, unloading, or where steps or handrails are involved. It is also good practice to collaborate with experienced drivers to glean and incorporate their feedback based on their practical day-to-day operational experience. When using tail-lift[7] operations incorporate tail-lift guard rails wherever feasible, there are several designs on the market.

Operational Management and Training

The senior H&S manager will have a NEBOSH qualification and is likely to have a raft of additional health, safety, and environmental accreditations that support the specific needs of the business, but it is recommended that every depot manager (or the most senior manager in a depot or satellite depot) receive requisite training in order to achieve the IOSH qualification, if the said manager does not already possess this qualification. There are an abundance of 3–4 day courses available on the market and as the senior manager on site employing many colleagues, multiple vehicle movements, all manner of general equipment and the premises to oversee, a minimum level of H&S awareness and knowledge of legislation and associated management responsibilities is fundamental to the safety of all employees and good governance to help protect the wider business, and having this accreditation will instil confidence in the DM and colleagues located at depot.

Notes

1. https://www.hse.gov.uk/statistics/industry/index.htm.
2. Heinrich, Herbert. 1931. *Industrial Accident Prevention*. New York: McGraw-Hill and Bird, Frank E. 1969. *The Safety Triangle Explained*.
3. Safety Stage. December 2020. All bout LTIR. https://safetystage.com
4. RIDDOR. Reporting of Injuries, Diseases and Dangerous Occurrences Regulations 2013. www.hse.gov.uk/riddor.
5. HSE 2013. ISBN. 9780717664733. Ergonomics and human factors at work.
6. hseblog.com. The 3 points of contact rule. April 2018.
7. HSE. SIM 05/2009/01. Reducing the risk of falls from tail-lifts.

Chapter 11

Continuous Improvement

Introduction

There is an abundance of literature regarding concepts designed to eradicate waste and optimise process performance, and whilst it is important to understand the various theories, this book aims to simplify the complex through simple and practical examples of workplace operating models; however, this chapter includes references for further reading should the reader wish to learn more about the origin of these concepts in greater detail.

Lean manufacturing principles were first conceived by Toyota during the 1930s with the expression "Lean" first developed by Krafcik[1] during the late 1980s and which have since been developed by many authors including Levinson.[2] Lean was developed as a concept in order to minimise waste and time within production processes, but many of these principles lend themselves to logistics operations as do the accompanying set of techniques that support process improvement and which are encapsulated under the umbrella of six sigma, which was pioneered by Motorola, who in 1993 registered six sigma a trademark; they (Motorola) proclaim that their relentless focus on defect elimination saved the company c17 billion dollars.

In parallel with these concepts during the 1980s–1990s, the theory of TQM (Total Quality Management)[3] emerged, the origins of which are not exact, but influenced by Ishikawa (Japan) and potentially the Department of Trade and Industry in the UK (1983) with the advent of the National "Quality Campaign." This campaign in part led to the emergence of the Standards bodies across part of Europe (UK, Germany, France, Belgium, and Turkey) and in the UK, the formulation of the BSI (British Standards Institute). TQM

DOI: 10.4324/9781003323822-11

is arguably the forerunner to the ISO9000 systems which in-part formulated the concept of SOPs (Standard Operating Procedures).

Interwoven with these concepts during this period were project management and performance management theories including SMART which was first coined by Dorcan but more widely attributed to Peter Drucker[4] applying the MBO (management by objectives) concept via a continual cycle, see Figure 11.1 illustrating the reward cycle, with each goal required to be objective, not subjective, and encompassing the SMART properties:

S	Specific
M	Measurable
A	Achievable
R	Relevant
T	Time bound

There are various iterations to the theme, and perhaps Shewhart's PDCA cycle[5] is the other much used method, see Figure 11.2. The concepts are similar, but the PDCA is process orientated rather than people focused, but

The reward cycle is as pertinent and useful today as first designed. Throughout this book a common thread is the need for managers to be data led, monitor and measure performance against plan / target and applying a drumbeat mechanism to maintain pace, focus and drive continual improvement in performance.

Figure 11.1   The Drucker reward cycle.

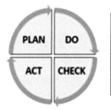

The standard PDAC cycle. Plan, identify the problem / opportunity, test various solutions with robust data, conduct analysis on the feedback and results (CHECK) and implement the optimum solution (ACT), and repeat the continuous improvement cycle

Figure 11.2   Shewhart's PDCA cycle.

the emphasis on requiring robust data and objective measurement of results common.

It is not necessary to introduce a plethora of "belted" six sigma trainers or introduce a significant "quality team" to a business in order to implement a continual improvement process, an entire industry has evolved from this platform, and whilst more relevant in a production setting, these concepts can be practically applied in the logistics setting without inflicting significant additional overhead costs.

The service standard, the percentage of services (drops) completed over received and planned services (drops), will reflect, in most cases, a contractual commitment the business has formally signed up to deliver on a customer-by-customer basis, this is an obligation not an aspiration and failure to achieve may invoke penalties or credits and sustained failure to achieve the targeted service goals may allow the customer to commence termination of proceedings. All other operational disciplines referenced in this book, and which aid improved productivity and output whilst minimising non-product time, are woven within a continual improvement cycle. Each element for example "reducing non-productive" in-depot time (Chapter 4) represents a journey that once management initiate, has no end. The journey commences with the formulation of a project team, relevant data, and the setting of an accurate baseline position, and thereafter incremental improvement is driven through repeatable cycles.

The responsibility of promoting and creating a collaborative management culture that both embraces and welcomes change, and energetically drive continuous improvement relentlessly across all facets of the operation must reside with senior operations management, if the desire to keep pushing productivity boundaries ever forward is not led from senior management applying common methodologies, the will to continually improve may wane, leaving only pockets of enthusiastic self-starting managers and these talented individuals may seek alternative career challenges in more forward-thinking companies if the organisation they are in stagnates.

Notes

1. Krafcik, John. 1990. *The Machine That Changed the World*. New York: Rawson Associates.
2. Levinson, William A. 2016. *Lean Management System*. Boca Raton, FL: CRC Press.

3. Martinez-Lorente, Angel R., Dewhurst, F., Frank, D., &Barrie, G. 1998. TQM Origins & Evolution of the Term. *The TQM Magazine*, Vol. 10. Bingley: MCB University Publishers Ltd.
4. Drucker, Peter. 1982. *The Practice of Management.* London: Heinemann.
5. Shewhart, W. A. 1986. *Statistical Methods from the Viewpoint of Quality Control.* New York Press. Originally published in 1939. Washington DC. Ronald, Moen, &Clifford, Norman. *Evolution of the PDCA cycle* (PDF). Graduate School of the Department of Agriculture. Westga.Edu.

Chapter 12

The Depot Manager Cadre

Introduction

The depot manager cadre represent the "nuts and bolts" of any depot route-based operation. This critical front-line management team have direct responsibility for the majority of employees and the day-to-day custodian-ship of fleet, customer service delivery whilst overseeing all-things "prem-ises" regarding their depot location; and whilst this tier is supported by and liaise daily with several functional departments including Fleet, Scheduling/Planning, HR, H&S, IT, Customer Services, Finance, and the senior Operations leadership team, this cadre is fundamental to delivering customer service in line with contracted service level agreements (SLAs), and with it ultimately business success or failure as perceived by the customer.

The role is broadly one of "general management" given the many and varied responsibilities associated with managing standalone premises, including location security, utilities consumption, stockholding, general maintenance, a myriad of supplier interfaces, and of course the health, safety, and well-being of the employees working at the depot. However, the DM's primary focus and "reason for being" is to deliver customer service excellence across the depot's geographical footprint in order to meet con-tractual SLA targets on a consistent basis, and crucially, delivered efficiently and at optimum cost.

Any business with a UK network of depots is likely to have a varied mix of building types which might be categorised as follows, small satellite depots operating ten or less vehicles, medium sized depots (11–30 vehicles), large (31–60), and very large depots (60+ with some having a fleet of 150 vehicles). When the numbers of warehouse, processing (machine operators), cleaning, and ancillary staff are considered, a very large depot may encompass a workforce of 300–400 employees.

The breadth of capability, seniority, experience, and gravitas required to lead a depot therefore varies considerably across the DM cadre and the breadth of leadership skills together with geographical location all have a bearing on a depot manager's renumeration package, so it is feasible that within a single UK business operating 20 plus depots with varying fleet numbers, the DM salary band is likely to reflect a broad range from £25,000 to £70,000 with the highest band reflecting a larger complex depot and or be located in London. Another factor that influences renumeration is the DM attrition rate which is likely to be nuanced geographically but related to large inner-city depots. DMs working in more rural areas often tend to reflect less of a flight risk and are often longer-serving employees whilst conversely DMs operating in inner-London may have shorter service due in part to the more challenging environment and higher employee attrition rates creating a transient workforce pool confined to a relatively small employee catchment area, and this employee landscape is a highly competitive merry-go-round providing drivers with a constant source of alternative job roles at similar or better rates of pay.

The DM structure and skills matrix is complex, remuneration may be further influenced by longevity of service with longer-serving managers sometimes paid less than newer external entrants who may have been enticed with more attractive packages to inject either additional logistics expertise found wanting internally, or to fulfil those inner-city large depot roles that internal candidates are less interested to try because of the historic stigma associated with an under-performing depot or lack of willingness regarding mobility. Businesses operating in the haulage and 3PL sectors are more likely to seek DMs with previous logistics leadership expertise and the DM cadre in these organisations is likely to have a reasonable level of logistics knowledge and may have received some logistics training during their career or as part of their education. The author's experience suggests that it is less common for route-based services-sector businesses to recruit DMs from a logistics background, the primary focus is more likely to seek candidates with knowledge of the core service (that which is provided, delivered, or installed at the customer's premises) or to habitually harvest "home-grown" internal "talent" and promote colleagues with strong core-service knowledge but who are unlikely to have formal depth of logistics expertise. There is some controversy as to who actually stated that "if you always do what you have always done, you will always get what you have always got" but the sentiment is pertinent in this context, more of the same is likely to inhibit innovation and productivity improvement that otherwise might be gained via the introduction of logistics principles. Arguably best business results are achieved by encompassing a range of skills and experiences within the DM cadre and to ensure that both core-service knowledge and logistical expertise coexist harmoniously.

Depot "tiering" (reflecting the range of depot types and sizes) provides, at face value, a natural business platform that will support personal management growth and career development; however, in practice, this often proves not to be the case; with DMs often being adverse, for all manner of reasons, to being "mobile" and willing to relocating themselves and families to a larger more challenging depot, even when a promotional prospect arises including enhanced salary packages, and this situation may give rise to business management promoting from the remnants of the depot team, but unless the business is willing to invest in requisite training and education (assuming an internal candidate is of suitable potential) and allow the budding manager and depot time to find its operational feet, this strategy may not provide the platform for operational success that the business and customer base demand.

In Chapters 1 and 8 ("People Management" and "KPIs, the Balance Scorecard, and Basic Financial Models"), the criticality of the DM cadre is discussed, and in Chapter 8 a suite of seven KPIs are identified which reflect core components of the DM role, and which spotlight the two central DM objectives of achieving customer service excellence at optimum efficiency. These seven KPIs are illustrated in Figure 12.1. Some businesses target DMs on revenue generation and depot net profitability, but these objectives incorporate responsibilities which are not solely related to the DM role and are at least partially out of the manager's control, the DM cannot entirely influence revenue trends or why a particular customer terminates a contract or withdrawers from a geography. The DM is unlikely to influence or determine customer pricing, and where businesses have a myriad of national customers, the internal allocation of revenue by customer may not exactly mirror the distribution of customer outlets to each depot. The DM's role and objectives are best focused on objective targets that he or she can directly control.

It is recommended that DMs are bonused in a way that inhibits DM attrition, maintains a competitive overall renumeration package, motivates a results-driven ethos that improves output and boost individual earnings, and is a scheme that represents a genuine win-win for both the business

DM KPIs	The KPI	Commentary	% of bonus allocation
Service	% of daily contracted / required drops / services completed	**Target 98% or higher.** (TBC by business). The business should target a higher % internally than is contracted with customers. An anchor KPI. All other depot KPIs are supporting achievement with this critical metric which defines the DM and depots performance, and how customers and the wider internal business judge depot and performance.	20%
Service	Ratio of complaints raised against Depot over total completed drops	**Target sub 0.05% of total drops** (TBC by business) The anchor Complaint KPI. Target TBC by business. If this KPI is indicating poor trends it is often representative of wider management & performance issues at Depot.	10%
People	% Attrition rate	**TBC by business.** An Anchor KPI. A guideline target is <30% for unqualified (non HGV) driving staff and <20% for qualified. Measure on rolling both 3 & 13 month trend basis. Poor attrition will increase training & recruitment costs & impact service.	15%
People	Paid hours vs. budgeted / planned hours	**Target zero variance** (unless volume growth occurs post budget & management agree reforecast). This is an "anchor" KPI and the results are almost entirely owned by the DM and team, if they manage drivers efficiently and without favour "unplanned" hours should be zero.	20%
Fleet	Up-time	**Target 96%+.** Calculated as total Fleet * working days in period reviewed over the total number of VOR days in period. This is an anchor KPI, and DMs can positively influence the overall % uptime if local time interface and manage their local workshops/garages efficiently and collaborate openly and enthusiastically with the business Fleet management team.	13%
Fleet	Number of vehicle RTAs or damage incidents	Target TBC by business per depot. DMs can impact this area positively or negatively, and it is a high cost, high business reputation area and if not meticulously managed costs can spiral out of control.	12%
Health & Safety	No. of Riddors*	**Target zero.** A Riddor is a lost time incident of 7 days or skeletal fracture or worse. Every Riddor requires investigation (see H&S Chapter). This is an anchor KPI which reflects the Depot H&S performance.	10%
			100%

Figure 12.1   Guideline DM KPIs aligned to bonus award if a bonus scheme operates.

and the manager. Further, the bonus should be mainly or fully dependent on individual depot performance rather than the output of the depot collective to prevent a high-performing DM from being penalised by poor peer performance.

The seven KPIs in Figure 12.1 include a guide percentage allocation of overall bonus potential on a per KPI basis to reflect the criticality of one KPI comparatively to others.

In businesses where DM bonus schemes exist, it is suggested that once the budgeted targets and KPIs are formally agreed, only a material change, not previously budgeted for, should be considered as justification to amend a bonus target to avoid unwarranted administration and endless "bargaining pleas" for what might be relatively minor changes to circumstance. Examples of a material change might include as a guideline:

1. A closure depot resulting in additional routes/drivers to a neighbouring depot and therefore significant revenues/costs being absorbed at the recipient depot, and this close project did not form part of the budgeting process.
2. A material customer (and associated volume of drops) that is won post budget and incorporated into the depot serviceable area and which cannot be integrated without the need for additional fleet and or drivers, the latter would reflect a reasonable adjustment; however, a portion of this new work (TBC) would be expected to be integrated with any additional resource as the increase in density will provide the basis to improve the drops-per-route productivity for the existing fleet, "offsetting" some of the received volume, so the adjustment must be tempered in this fashion.
3. A material customer (and requisite drop volume) is lost, and this loss is (a) not due to poor service from the depot in question (if this were the case no adjustment should be warranted) and (b) the loss was not already reflected in the budget process.

The business should periodically conduct comparative analysis (at least annually) to compare DM salaries with peer groups in competitive companies within similar geographies. However, the business may need to expedite this process if specific circumstances dictate, for example a service company moves into the area and opens a similar or large depot presenting an opportunity for the DM to improve their package and or prospects.

Depot service and productivity performance can recede rapidly in the absence of a DM, and it is imperative therefore to minimise any period of absence due to either prolonged sickness or a DM exiting the business for whatever reason without the organisation having the time or ability to have implemented a smooth succession plan. A substitute of some description should be in-situ within a week of departure latest, either the second in command at depot (2IC) from within the depot or from a neighbouring depot standing-in temporarily; or if necessary, the RM should work from the depot temporarily and assume the DM role in response to a needs-must scenario, it is important that senior management treat the absence of DM in any depot as a business priority. That said, it is paramount that every DM is of the highest calibre relative to the size and complexity of the depot that he or she is leading, mediocre managers produce mediocre results and are likely, at times of challenge, for example during peak trading season, or during transitional projects (e.g. significant new business win, depot integration, or large business project such as new PDA or IT rollout) that their inherent frailty will be exposed, and depot service or the project at hand may fail locally and rapidly. Where a DM's performance is found wanting, and the said DM is unable to improve personal and depot performance having received support and guidance and reasonable time to resolve performance and output to the required standard, then senior management need to performance manage until exit.

Task-Force Manager

In businesses with 15 plus depots configured nationally, a concept worthy of consideration is the recruitment of a national fully mobile task-force manager, reporting to the COO or Operations Director. This role is ostensibly without portfolio and the candidate of a calibre and experience of a large depot DM and be trained to be fully conversant with all depot related functions, tasks and responsibilities, and IT core systems. The individual will be trained to the ISOSH standard. The individual must be fully mobile, flexible, and willing travel away-from-home on a permanent basis as required; in a business with a national configuration of depots, the recommended home location (from experience) would be Birmingham centric, or in the home-counties corridor between Birmingham and North West London. The primary aim of this role is to cover any DM vacancy, and where practical to provide holiday and sickness cover across the depot network.

Whilst it is not straightforward to recruit a fully mobile individual, the salary may need to be higher than a peer DM that is static, but it is easier to recruit one such role and cheaper than third-party interim managers paid a day rate and with zero business knowledge, and less disruptive than pulling managers from one depot to cover another. Additionally, there are always several innovative productivity related or other operational projects that are in-flight that are the better for focused support, and when not actively "standing-in" as DM, the task-force manager can be leading or supporting these projects to help further his or her experience and career.

Glossary

2IC: Second in command at depot. The immediate assistant to the depot manager (DM), sometimes referred to as "service manager," "department manager," or "operations manager."

3PL: Third-party logistics provider.

AWOL: Absent without leave. An expression used when a colleague fails to notify management before the start of shift that he or she is unable to attend work for that day. This absence is neither planned nor known of by management.

CIT: Cash in transit. Businesses that collect and deliver physical cash (pound notes, cheques, and coins) to/from customers.

Contract: Employee contract of employment. The contract will outline the basic terms and conditions of employment including place of work, contracted hours of work, remuneration, holiday entitlement, etc. This document is usually supplemented by a Company Handbook, the latter providing guidance on procedures and more detailed company policies not always incorporated into the contract (for example The Grievance Procedure).

Direct staff: Front-line colleagues including drivers, driver assistants, warehouse and stores or stock controllers, technicians, engineers. Direct staff are those that "touch" or handle the company product or goods and or physically interface with customers at customer premises.

DM: Depot manager. The most senior manager at a depot. Sometimes referred to as Operations Centre Manager. Within this cadre there is a wide range of salary and responsibility depending on the size and complexity of the depot.

Employee Handbook: Supplementary to the employee contract, the Handbook details company policies, and procedures, and is a reference document for both management and employees which is periodically updated and re-issued.

Establishment: The budgeted and approved planned number of employees, including drivers and warehouse staff that is required at each depot in order to process the volume demand. Each depot will have a unique driver establishment to satisfy the drop demand across the depot's geographical service area. The driver requirement is fluid, not static, and may fluctuate throughout the year to mirror changes in volume throughput including seasonal peaks. Calculating the establishment number is a science not guesswork, and the number must be approved by senior management, setting the correct driver establishment is a core management task that will influence depot costs and customer service.

ETA and ETF: Estimated time of arrival/attendance and estimated time to finish/complete.

EV: Electric commercial vehicle.

FCV: Fuel cell vehicles (incorporating pressurised hydrogen cells).

HGV: Heavy goods vehicle with a gross vehicle weight (GVW) of plus 3.5 tonnes.

Indirect staff: "Backroom" staff that work in depots that manage and or support direct staff, such roles may include the DM, other depot management, depot administrators, planners/schedulers, premise cleaners (if PAYE).

KPI: Key performance indicator. A metric used to measure actual and trend performance against plan/target.

NDC/RDC: National Distribution Centre (a single warehouse location that distributes goods and product nationally) or Regional Distribution Centre, one of several strategically located large depots that distribute goods and services to a defined regional geographical area. The latter is used where more high-density fast-moving product is required in significant volume and often where service lead-times are short, an example would be to service a network of supermarkets across a defined geographical area from a single RDC.

LCV: Light commercial vehicle (commercial vans of less than 3.5 tonnes).

On-cost: Additional costs payable by the company beyond the basic salary include National Insurance (NI) contributions and pension contributions, the value may differ depending on contractual terms and conditions but usually for direct staff on-cost as a percentage of base pay will be in the range of 13%–15%.

OT: Overtime hours and or payments. Overtime reflects additional hours worked above the basic contracted hours per day and or per week (basic hours tend to be in the range of 35–45 hours weekly for direct employees). Overtime hours may be paid at a basic rate (a flat rate equalling basic pay) or may attract supplementary payment, and this additional rate varies from company to company and is likely to depend on the day of the week worked, for example extra weekday hours may be paid at 1:25, hours worked on a Saturday at 1:5 ("time and one-half") and for hours worked on Sunday or a bank holiday at *2 ("double-time"), with some companies paying bank holidays at 2 + and providing a day off in lieu or *3 (triple time). The OT rates vary considerably from company to company with the origins of these payments set historically, and where unions exist, the latter will almost always have a negotiating influence regarding the rates and conditions surrounding overtime payments.

MHE: Mechanical handling equipment. For example, forklift-trucks and smaller pallet trucks (hand push or "ride-on").

MPG: Miles per gallon. The average miles driven per gallon consumed per vehicle model type. Some companies now use KPG (kilometres per gallon).

NDA: A non-disclosure agreement. The HR department would produce this document which is applied when sharing confidential information to a party (colleague or third-party) but require the information to remain confidential and to ensure that the individual signing the NDA will not disclose said information to third-parties. An NDA is often used in a settlement agreement (SA) as part of a complicated employee dismissal case, or with the participants that are going to be involved in "special" business projects or preparation for a project which is confidentiality, of a sensitive nature that may impact colleague future employment, for example an exploratory review and business case formulating the rationale and impact as to whether a specific depot should be closed.

NPS: Net promoter score. A formal structured customer service feedback process that companies deploy to glean meaningful data on what their customers think and feel about the service they receive from the business; this process is formal, thorough, detailed, and encompasses all areas of business activity including operational service, employee attitude, invoicing, credit control, sales staff, and selling methodology. If the process is implemented robustly and with employee "ownership," the impact to service performance and business processes can be material and have a positive and lasting impact.

PPE: Personal protective equipment. Protective clothing issued by the company to protect employees whilst conducting their duties, PPE will usually include, but not limited to, boots, uniform (including any heavy-duty winter coats), gloves, ear defenders, goggles, hard hats, etc. Some of these items may be specialist in type due to the specific working environment or products/materials being handled by staff. Examples might include stab vests (CIT drivers) or anti-stab gloves (clinical hygiene collection workers). The wearing of PPE is usually mandatory and used in conjunction with standard operating procedures (SOPs) providing instructions on what PPE is required when conducting a specific task.

R&M: Fleet, MHE or premise "repair and maintenance." Referred to in this book with regard the R&M of commercial vehicles. Fleet R&M may be completed by in-house (company owned and company operated workshops/garages) or via external third-party R&M suppliers.

RAG: Red, Amber, Green. A "traffic-light" colour mechanism applied to tables, charts, etc. and which depict an easy-read visual representation of either high-low risk or good-poor performance, each company may interpret to varying degree.

RTA: Road traffic accident. In the context of this book, it reflects an accident involving a company commercial vehicle.

RTW: Return-to-work "interview." Upon returning to work following a period of absence or sickness, the employee should receive a formal return-to-work interview before work commences to assess their well-being, ensure their fitness to return to work at the workplace, and understand the root cause of the absence.

SA: Settlement agreement. Produced by the HR department with support from the Legal team (either in-house or external solicitor). The SA may be deployed in complex employee dismissal or "exit" cases, or to ensure confidentiality before and during special or sensitive business projects.

SLA: Service level agreement. Forming part of a contract between customer and company, a section of the contract will contain the SLA(s) which set out the contracted or targeted service level standards that the company supplying the services will agree to maintain (i.e., 98% of service drops to be conducted on time – delivered on the agreed day(s) within an agreed service window e.g., 10.00–11.00). SLAs may also contain penalty clauses that are triggered if the SLA is not complied with by the supplier, with a subsequent payment of a credit to the customer; some contracts may incorporate a termination clause if the contracted service level is not achieved or is repeatedly failed (for example three successive periods of service not meeting SLA and where rectification has failed).

SME: Small medium enterprise. Each country has a slightly different categorisation of what constitutes an SME; in the UK, an SME is a business with less than 250 employees. SMEs represent the overwhelming majority of operating businesses in the UK. In a logistics business or route-based service-sector company, the customer profile may differ greatly and will, in part, determine the organisational and depot structure; for example a company supplying a single large "blue-chip" corporation such as Marks & Spencer's will require a quite different logistical infrastructure to a service company providing services to tens of thousands of customers. Some businesses will provide services to hundreds of thousands of customers and in these cases the customer base will often have a diverse range of customer types from the SME to the large international corporate organisation, with the split often in the range of 70%–90% SME customers and 10%–30% corporate customers.

SOP: Standard operating procedure. A formal documented procedure written for employees to understand how to perform a specific task. The SOP should be readily accessible, usually situated at the location where the task is conducted, it must be "current" (with updated versions maintained and date-stamped) and in easy-to-read language with pertinent photographs and or instructional pictures. In the context of this book which focuses largely on driver colleagues, the SOP(s) are likely to be carried in the vehicle (place of work), be laminated (to protect against spills and dirt) within a ring binder so drivers can easily access the SOP relevant to the task they are about to conduct whilst on-location.

YTD: Year-to-date. When measuring performance either financially or via non-financial KPIs (e.g. drops per driver route, or a depot's absence % trend), a business will measure and review by accounting periods and measure performance YTD to provide a balanced picture of performance which is both current and trend. Therefore, if a business is reviewing Period 4, it will measure the individual period, and the trend position of periods 1–4 (the YTD position).

Index

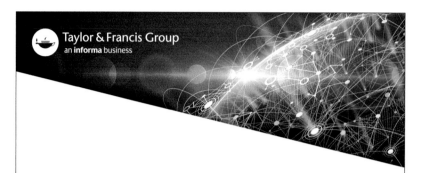